Free Verse Editions

Edited by Jon Thompson

Praise for Valerio Magrelli's Writing

"Valerio Magrelli . . . represents, to this reader at least, a new moment in Italian poetry. In the good-natured ease with which he shows off his mastery of the traditional tools of his trade, and the elegant way he lets the reader know he knows that writing is about writing, he advertises his membership in an international con-fraternity whose current English-language practitioners include Mark Strand and, especially, Paul Muldoon. Magrelli, a scholar of French literature and an experienced translator, is obsessed by the "translation" involved in all writing, and thus by language games that reveal the complex inner life of words. . . . Language itself is, naturally, one of this poet's prime subjects; Dante, he tells us, in a typically cheeky, inspired acrostic, is the "DNA of poETry," and the structure of his terza rima is the literary double-helix that contains "the future of the mother tongue" in the same way that the ur-poet's name magically incorporates life's ultimate building block. I know of no other Italian poet today who writes with such a capacious grasp of the enormous, still-to-be-discovered potentialities of the great treasure-house of Italian. Here is a writer whose energy and gifts open a doorway onto an expansive future."

—Jonathan Galassi

Praise for Vanishing Points

What a gift, this superb selection of work [*Vanishing Points*] from the glorious, ingenious, and essential Valerio Magrelli. For the last twenty five years, in poems, notebooks, fragments, dreams, daydreams, Magrelli has ardently pursued the metaphysics of the uncanny, where catching a glimpse, a trace, of one's double, is the only way to find the way to one's self. Like spirit-photographs which, after multiple exposures, make what appears to not exist visible, these poems find language between sleeping and waking, the manifest and the un-manifest, to draw us into that hushed zone where the other world in our world emerges. Each stunning poem is a darkroom in which this magic occurs, where the visitor in each of us shows up, is opened to light, and exposed. It is powerful, poignant, courageous work, and full of lambent joy.

—Jorie Graham

Valerio Magrelli's poetry quietly sneaks up on the reader; at first it often seems to be translucently simple, readily accessible. However, the simplicity is deceptively complex, and the accessibility soon demands a deeper, more intense engagement. Our ears, minds, and hearts are put to the task of receiving the perceptual and linguistic subtleties of his verse, and we are all the better for it. *Vanishing Points* is a marvelously wrought book of translations that opens the moving intelligence of a unique poetic voice to English-language readers. I, for one, am deeply grateful.

—Rebecca West

CONDOMINIUM OF THE FLESH

Valerio Magrelli

Translated by Clarissa Botsford

Parlor Press
Anderson, South Carolina
www.parlorpress.com

Parlor Press LLC, Anderson, South Carolina, 29621

Printed in the United States of America
S A N: 2 5 4 - 8 8 7 9

Library of Congress Cataloging-in-Publication Data

Magrelli, Valerio, 1957-
[Nel condominio di carne. English]
Condominium of the flesh / Valerio Magrelli ; translated by Clarissa Botsford.
pages cm. -- (Free Verse Editions)
ISBN 978-1-60235-748-8 (pbk. : acid-free paper)
I. Botsford, Clarissa, translator. II. Title.
PQ4873.A3624N4513 2016
851'.914--dc23
2015029128

Cover design by Leonardo Magrelli
Printed on acid-free paper.

Parlor Press, LLC is an independent publisher of scholarly and trade titles in print and multimedia formats. This book is available in paperback and ebook formats from Parlor Press on the World Wide Web at http://www.parlorpress.com or through online and brick-and-mortar bookstores. For submission information or to find out about Parlor Press publications, write to Parlor Press, 3015 Brackenberry Drive, Anderson, South Carolina, 29621, or email editor@parlorpress.com.

Contents

CONDOMINIUM OF THE FLESH

I

My past is an illness contracted in infancy. That's why I've decided to try and understand how and why it all happened. These clinical notes make no attempt to create an anatomical theatre of my body; they are rather a sequence of photographic stills. What counts is the flow of frames, the creature squirming out of its skin vibrating within me, the mutations of its form among other forms: blood vessels, mollusk shells, beehives, highway junctions, bird skeletons, floating crystals and helixes. There's no plot, just a plot against me: an exercise in the pathos of pain. There's no theory, just a story of small catastrophes, each played out within the intergalactic space of the flesh.

The expression 'somatization' refers to the way the body responds to internal pressure, but what I explore here is the concept of 'psychization', when an instinct is made conscious the way an object can be magnetized. I'm talking about very low levels of energy: how does our mental system react to the transformations of its scaffolding? Why does hair cling to the comb that has torn it out? A delicately translucent cobweb, seaweed vacillating weakly in undersea currents.

I ride a wave that dissolves under me, and as it dissolves pushes me away. I ride a wave that crests just ahead of me, perennially out of reach. I ride a current that bolts through my flesh and strikes somewhere else. I ride a current that is flesh. Wrinkles and creases form. I surf cells.

I will not make a list of all my ailments, which are anyway insignificant. I will only mention those where the metamorphic nature of the organism is most evident. You see the foam on the wave, and—for at least a second—the ray of light that hits the tight skin of the water looks like it's rolling the wave forward. These notes are *tableaux vivants* as well as graphs and charts. Why did I go to all this trouble? "To find out whether per chance I am an even more complex and fearsome monster than Typhon".[1]

II

Exfancy

The malfunctioning of my system was a guiding star, a psychopomp[2] escorting me to the afterlife and providing a running commentary while doing so. (I have the same relationship with my ailments that a Sunday painter has with art: I'm by no means a professional, but I have great deal of experience and some talent).

Here is an early photogram. A bewildered family huddled in the doctor's surgery, as if in hiding from King Herod's soldiers. It was my first trip to the eye specialist. Squinting at the chart with its illuminated hieroglyphics—a Rosetta stone heralding a long descent into twilight—with the phoropter still on (a black steel octopus-like machine into which different lenses were inserted and then rotated in order to test my eyesight), the doctor told me to get up and go, just as I was, with the whole contraption still on my nose.

By the time I realized he was joking it was too late to dissipate a sense of nauseating enucleation. This wasn't an illness in itself; it was, rather, the underlying trigger for every manifestation that was to follow. I recognized that I was condemned to live behind an iron mask, or, like a building under renovation, behind the scaffolding covering its façade.

But I was prepared. Now I had the prosthesis through which to gaze at, and through, an infinite number of further prostheses. These protruding antennae with carefully calibrated heavy glass discs, these scourges for eye-browed creatures—I would wear them as radio transmitters of disease. The frame was mounted: the show could begin.

III

The first rehearsal was to take place a few days later. At school in his new glasses (no longer the oculist's test lenses, but still intrusive and fusional, an extraneous body devouring his face), the young pupil, who could never sit still, was sent out of the classroom. Shut out on the terrace. How long was I out there, on my own, exposed to the heat and the light, held captive in that punishing eerie? There was no more than a pane of glass to separate me from the other kids' ridicule as they ganged up against me in the cool penumbra of the classroom—a Nymph's cavern. An hour, perhaps two, must have gone by, but time seemed to dilate unbelievably in the dilated world of a person who, for the first time, found himself behind a lens, like an insect under a microscope. A spasmodic tension deformed the outlines of things, subjecting them to an extenuating topology of vision.

Stared at from behind the French window, trapped on a tiny stage, and at the same time forced into a painful traction of his sight, the victim of this torture of prying eyes was first and foremost tormented by his own. In his hypertrophic eye the world around him stretched and shrank, bent and oscillated, while the June afternoon sunlight never let up. I was struck down by sunstroke, which embraced me sweetly as I fainted. I actually saw darkness coming, standing out on the balcony of the sky, casting its shadow slowly over my face like an eyelid, the last thing to separate me from the things that surrounded me.

(Another fainting fit. A ferry, a storm, so much retching my body was incapacitated. I lost consciousness but was still awake! I could 'see myself' insulting people around me. Swearing at them for forty minutes, determined not to sacrifice anything to the pale mother-of-pearl god of the dank depths. The trance was opium-like. My out of body experience was self-induced, its origin brutally dietary, stoked by giant donuts.)

(Yet another fainting episode. On holiday, after a long Mass celebrated in the frozen crypt of a country church, an outdoor meal hastily and greedily dispatched when the sun was at its zenith. I had just enough time to look around me before night fell, a darkness of the soul—at least that's what it felt like—while my head emptied suddenly, and my blood drained eagerly to my extremities, bolus by bolus.)

IV

Whoever invented six-thirty pm? Who could have conceived of such a lethally boring hour? Where did this blip of time come from, breaking up the day, fracturing it, obliging it to slow down and interrogate itself? It's Thursday, dinner is still a long way off, an indefinite blur on the horizon. The warmth created by lunch has worn off, leaving a state of hypothermic torpor reflected in the cup of cold coffee left on the shelf. A muddy puddle, a cataplasm. The day the sun died, St Lucy's day. Darkness. Work languishes. The old cannot draw to a close and the new cannot come to life. The new cannot come to life. This is the still point at which I was born, in the backwash of the world. It was a Thursday at six-thirty pm, while on television it was time for a commercial break. Stasis. I feel I am the child of stagnation and of hypochondria. Born, like an upside-down black Venus, from the muddy backwaters of the afternoon's "spurious infinity"[3].

V

I've worn glasses ever since. That is, I exhibit that which I lack; I certify the figure that separates me from normal eyesight. Unbidden, I declare the degree of my short-sightedness in a resigned request for transparency. That could be why I still associate the sensation with the day—the only day ever—I was forced to wear bobble socks. Why? What sacred rite did I have to celebrate? What did those hideous dancing testicles signify? What sin did I have to expiate by submitting myself to such an embarrassing spectacle? It takes so little, an embroidered design, a little anchor maybe, and an angel wielding a flaming sword chases us out of Eden, without a stitch on us—except for our bobble socks.

VI

Contact lenses are not even worth mentioning. Friends doubled over with their heads in their hands and their retinas sliced apart; others feeling about on the floor only to discover the foreign body is behind their eye-bulb, that is inside their body. (What does a lens do inside a body? The bloody mass must sneakily take possession of it, and then refuse to let it go; it probably goes around with it, like Caliban with a monocle). No way will I resort to contacts. Rather the laser, the gold needle that cauterizes and stitches our charcoal-broiled crystalline lens until sight is restored with brand new bling. But surgery can wait for now…

VII

The great continent of the ears—a sonorous gate, a hearing shell. Early attempts at diving have left me with strange vibrations in my eardrums: when a train approaches, when someone shouts down the telephone, when an unexpected sound wave hits the air. Whistling, hissing, giddiness and premonitions of sounds (a Sioux with his ear on the ground detecting the first trembling of the train as it runs along the curves of the shining metal tracks). Strange noises in my Eustachian tube led to the repugnant unearthing of earwax—the organic equivalent of toxic waste. Deforming sediments of that lethal deposit, a magic bog of Knorr stock cubes.

There were two possible solutions. The first was hydraulic, inspired by Hercules's fifth labor—the cleaning of the Augean stables. An infinitely long syringe of warm water washing through the convolutions of my ears: a deep plunge, a swooning of the senses, scuba diving inside myself with no point of arrival, an orgasmic dizziness. A Water Park! But there's always the risk of a ruptured eardrum (might it be precisely this risk that stimulates my narcotic abandon to the maternal and regressive flow of water?).

The second was mechanical: digging out the mess with tweezers, pincers, tongs. A rotten harvest of infected vegetation. Ear spelunking: a dwarf—complete with head-lamp—lowering himself into the depths of the mines. Black jewels, bacilli, a purge, a septic tank that reveals what we really are: producers of sludge.

VIII

Addenda for the ears

a) first acoustic study

Olive green Fiat Croma, license plate RM 25926X, Bright red Suzuki, license plate RM 57660V, metallic grey Mercedes 300, license plate CE72868V. My desk is strewn with bits of paper, every shred a number plate. Like my heroic toy Mounties in their red serge, I am on night duty—but there's no forest visible from my watchtower. What I see is a road junction, and I live in expectation of the next tremor.

Except that this was not a one-off shock to the system but an interminable draining of my veins, something like a wellhead that has been drilled for years when a sudden geyser, a plume of crude oil, gushes out of it—the spray of a gigantic buried whale coming up for air. Hydrocarbons, putrescent essences stoking the machine room: this is the substance of the sound that was spurting out of the black car with a Palermo number plate. A sound-secretion that was like mineral oil, industrial crude, infinitely renewable deposits.

It would be no easy task to stop the noise, I thought to myself, my mind rushing to powerful, magical weapons of destruction: explosives, death beams. In the end I decided to resort to a trick I had seen at the movies to keep cars from starting. It wouldn't solve the problem of the noise, of course, but my revenge would be worth the trouble. What was required? Quite simply, a raw potato shoved into the exhaust pipe. It would be a good laugh when, the next day, the car spluttered and failed to start. Thus, dressed as a saboteur, I went down into the street and took action.

Back home, pleased with my accomplished mission, I take off my resistance fighter's garb while the roar of fossil fuel continues unaffected by my actions. Suddenly I am overcome by a doubt, which insinuates its way into my appeased fantasies. How did the scene in that film end? Am I mistaken, or didn't the car explode? Didn't the plot take an unpredictable turn? Am I right in thinking that the blocked exhaust pipe let off a spark that set the car on fire, carbonized its inhabitants, and created a massive crater in the middle of the road? That's it. I'm throwing my clothes back on, I'm back on the street tackling the car's exhaust pipe. Lying flat on my back, my tools a knife and fork, I spend several useless minutes trying in vain to release the gastric blockage. I try and hook my prey. I wait, at the mouth of the exhaust pipe of the night. A fisherman trying to catch Zen potatoes.

b) Second Acoustic Study

Last night things went quite well: it only happened twice. The first time was at around three, the second at four, in the morning. But it wasn't like the other times. I'm sleeping, wrapped up in my heat, and, while I'm dreaming, something like a wrench starts twisting the oneiric little film round. It sends it off kilter. Extraneous figures try to introduce themselves into the interstices, between one frame and another, splicing the images until the reel blocks, the film melts, an ectoplasm invades the whole screen, the projection is held up, the audience boos and whistles, and I am awake. A radio. It was a radio that knocked the walls of my sleep down with its deranged repetition of a little ditty and a heartbeat of conga drums. For miles around me no other human being appears to be disturbed by it. Unhappy product of an evolutionary leap of the species that I am, I seem to be the only person in the neighborhood to be equipped with a sense of hearing.

Everything in the square from where the music is rising is still. So I get my tools out and go down onto the road where the cars are parked. There's no sign of life, but the sound is loud and clear, unperturbed. Until I find it. The sound I find is an autonomous presence, a thing in itself. We find each other. It is coming from an empty car. The radio is off, but there is music emanating from it. A ghost ship that has travelled through the ages on a mission to come and wake me up. It could be an excessively fine-tuned alarm, or simply an electrostatic state of grace, and yet there is no mistaking it: this car sings solo. I feel the same sense of awe a savage must have felt when faced with a tree trunk struck by lightning. The idea that some superior power must have caused the fire.

And yet, faced by the flames I don't seem to feel any emotion. I have nothing I want to cook. Music does not make a barbeque. So I slice the antenna in two with a sharp twist of my pincers. The music stops. At least, it stops long enough for me to get back to bed and fall asleep again. Then there's a car alarm. I don't need to look for it, I know where the wail is coming from. I know that an amputation leaves its mark, not immediately perhaps, but in the long run. And here it is, braying away.

There's no mystery this time, no captured melodic sound wave or faint cosmic fluctuation. It is a Primal Scream. In one way at least my search was lucky because the car door wasn't locked. I could climb in and work in peace. I'll never know if it was beginner's luck or white magic. I cut everything. I swear, I spliced everything that remotely resembled a wire. One lead after another, but the Scream went on. And I went on too, bent over the open hood, to no end. I even cut the little ribbon which tied a horn-shaped amulet onto the rear-view mirror, but, as I feared, this didn't help at all. I cut the water pipe and spliced the fuel injector, and as I walked away from the mess, giving up, I looked back at the car. It resembled a tangled ball of wool, but it was still whining miserably.

They say, unravel the problem and you'll find the solution… well, I didn't find the solution. The city police did, after an hour-long inspection, as dawn rose over the shapeless pile of scrap. The noise bled out like an animal butchered in the kosher tradition; it was a state-endorsed execution. And I'm still wondering what that wailing soul was looking for, what it wanted me to do.

c) THIRD ACOUSTIC STUDY

My name is Ernesto Calindri—star of the famous Cynar liquor advertisement in which I sit and sip from the bitter cup with traffic whirling noisily all around me. Let me try and describe the Ptolemaic nature of the harsh battle I have fought for years against noise. I am at the centre of infinitely noisy orbits, that poor St. Sebastian of my brain the axis of a revolving hula hoop.

I once lived in a quiet alley. One summer's night a low grumble summoned me, sweetly, then exhaustingly, insinuating itself into my consciousness. It was a hidden, feral sound that teased out and exacerbated my insomnia and finally prevented sleep from taking place. I went downstairs only to find it was not an animal at all, but a bewitched entry phone—'bewitched' not as in 'magic' but as in 'stuck', like a broken record. To put it simply, there was an electrical contact. It groaned out of nowhere, and there was nothing anyone could do about it. Was I supposed to let this noise go on? Was I supposed to listen to it flapping in the air like bunting, or a flag? No, I was not. I rushed back to fetch bandages, cotton gauze and sticky plasters.

Now, in the halo of a lamp post, I suture the sonorous wound, pulling together the two folds. I stem the pitiful hemorrhage even as it calls out to me. I dull the sound as much as it can be dulled. The entry phone has turned into a monstrous growth.

It sticks out from the door jamb, a concave mass of cotton wool and adhesive tape, casting its own little regulation shadow. The moan? Suffocated. But not for long. Have the stitches torn? The mouth of the wound must have re-opened; there's blood plasma draining out of it. Slowly, of course, slowly to start with. But it's getting faster. The flow is increasing, and it's denser than before. Gush, you low-life! Gush away, sound outlet, sticky lymph, secretion, stem, beanstalk! Ha! That's the trick—for a beanstalk you need an axe.

I'm no longer the well-meaning doctor I was a minute before. I am Jack the wood-cutter on a rampage against noise. With sharp heaves of my axe I cut down the hissing tree. A vivid image: a blade penetrating the anodized aluminum and revealing the gills of the microphone (delicate, curled, parallel). In a flash the dark wire is spliced, dark night, Irma's injection[4].

Silence. There's no uvula under the soft palate, no tonsils, nor tongue in the smoking mouth, which gapes wide open once the cover with the buttons and the names has been ripped off. All I need now is a teaspoon to check for a sore throat. Open wide and say 'Ah, …' There's a good girl; now let me go back to sleep.

D) FOURTH ACOUSTIC STUDY

This could be the reason
Why they take their silencers off their Vespas,
Turn their radios up to full volume,

And a minimal saint can expect rockets—noise
a counter-magic, a way of saying
"Boo" to the Three Sisters: "Mortals we may be
But we are still here!"[5]

Do I need to explain that noise, even in its more organized forms, belongs to the same family as excrement? People who like making noise in public clearly derive an organic sort of pleasure from doing so. The problem is that everyone else has to suffer; everyone else has to deal with the effects of this metabolic totalitarianism. As Kant says, "Music has a certain lack of urbanity about it. For owing chiefly to the character of its instruments, it scatters its influence abroad to an un-called for extent through the neighborhood, and thus, as it were, becomes obtrusive and deprives others, outside the musical circle, of their *freedom* [...]. The case is almost on a par with the practice of regaling oneself with a perfume that exhales its odors far and wide. The man who pulls his perfumed handkerchief from his pocket gives a treat to all around *against their will*."[6]

So, use your headphones. Pick up a spade and shovel away this pile of fecal sounds, this peristalsis of cadenced vibrations. Every sound is a pang, a tummy rumble, diarrheic intestinal noises and gastric juices. There will come a day when silence will be the only sacred thing worth venerating, when respect for others will be shown by revering the communion bread of quiet, the only wafer of community life. And when anyone who produces noise, anyone who imposes his presence on others uninvited, will be the scapegoat of the whole tribe.

Sinners will not be sent to live in caves, mutilated or killed. Far from it. Their punishment will be to have their sense of hearing sharpened beyond measure so that they can appreciate from close up what it means to have their hearing violated. They will be forced to listen. They will be able to hear a light cough or intake of breath in a neighbors' house, the sound of a finger turning the heating on, a loud click and then the flow of the current through the endless circuits of the system, the echoing boom of a CD being put back in its case, the loud clack of the plastic box as it envelopes the little musical bomb, a gateway of a B52 loaded with silent coffins...

But they will not be able to hear music. They will only be able to feel deep sound waves in their hearts, beating in the fragile armor of their chest cavities. A sound-blow, its shape dilated, the outline of an atomic mushroom rising on the horizon with a blinding radioactive bass. Nothing else.

E) FIFTH ACOUSTIC STUDY

The Sixties. One hot August afternoon, in a parked car, searching for something on the back shelf, I am amazed to find six 45 rpm records completely warped by the heat. Sound altered by light, topological models of galactic structures. Anyway, they can't be played. Vinyl deformed by the light of childhood.

IX

A white beach. Marching with other children my age in almost military formation along the clear, still, incredibly blue shoreline. My eyes take in the morning seascape, glittering in the terse summer breeze. The reason I am pausing to describe the beauty of the scene is in order to understand how it connects with what was to follow.

The focus is on my skin; the temporary adieu it was giving to the rest of my body. Yes, because while I was wandering about in that paradise of bright sunlight, that same sunlight was working fervidly on my skin. Readying me for a feast. No, readying me, period. It flayed the skin, separating it from the flesh (honey-coated Peking duck), and with its fluted breath it blew music, or liquid, or serum—who knows what?—into the wound. That evening, in my tent, my back was a three-dimensional map with mountain ranges in relief.

This was the first trophy in a long track-record of sunburns. The next day I had to go out protected by bandages. I went on to see my face detach itself slowly like a funeral mask (a nursery rhyme I used to chant talked about Apollo's son, Apelle, who made a ball out of chicken-skin). Later again, in Delphi of all places, Apollo's island, cloaked like an Orthodox monk, I would feel my sun-burnt, itching hands become the incandescent, magic forks of a diviner's rod.

As for my feet, the adventure reminds me of Artemidorus's *Oneirocritica.*[7] I can still see an uncle of mine smiling to himself on his slow, solitary, barefoot walk along the blazing sand of the beach. No human being, no living creature, no plant, no mineral would be able to tolerate contact with the fiery sand, already nearly turned to glass. He took life calmly, living on a war pension, a survivor of the Russian campaign who suffered severe frostbite in his feet and hands. Cold, neoclassical marble, ice on fire.

This is all to say that in those days of relentless heat I used to enjoy lying curled up in the shade and observing his profile, deep in thought like the sculptor Canova. One day, a young girl appears in a dream and bends over me. She doesn't kiss me; no, she strokes my foot with a sharpened blade. Or is it Psyche waking Cupid with her burning drop of oil? I wake up with a start to find a gang of friends around me guffawing. Someone has stuck a lit cigarette in between my sun-burnt toes.

X

Seven years later, I suffered a sudden and immense swelling of my scrotum. A symbolic elephantiasis: armor-plated, totemic, purplish skin, veined like parchment. Devastating subcutaneous hot flashes. I was staying with my uncle and aunt for Christmas, and as we all sat piously at dinner I had to excuse myself repeatedly to splash cold water onto the inflamed area. Nessus's burning underpants.[8] My skin fizzled and smoked like pork crackling with every jet of water.

The agony didn't ease until the next day when a doctor prescribed calendula. It took seconds. The swelling went down as if I had opened a cage and let the beast out. The only sign of the animal's passage was a rash of little blisters trailing downwards, right down to my feet, following its escape path. The beast had returned to the jungle.

XI

I was an adult when I broke my arm. After thirty days of immobility I expected the limb to look pale and sickly, diaphanous and ghost-like. I couldn't have been more wrong. It lay there, practically identical to before. Was everything back to normal? Not at all. This illusionary normalcy concealed a new metamorphosis: a terrible smell. It was when they took off the cast that the Genie appeared. All I had to do was rub my skin, like Aladdin's lamp, and the spirit was before me, ready to do my will. A light rub of my wrist was enough to summon from that arm, that unassuming arm, a gargantuan stinking ectoplasm. I had expected something of the kind, but not that creature, not the Genie. It wasn't just the unbearable stench; there was a further ultra-dermal dimension. And I soon understood why.

In those few weeks the skin had not only rotted. In one spot, between the thumb and the index finger, it had started to decompose, macerating slowly and turning flaky. But more than that, it felt like perhaps its moment had come. To put it simply, it was putrefying—or preparing to do so. Preparing to go away somewhere.

I had never smelt anything like it. It belonged to the cheese family, those cheeses ripened in dark caves. No, this was even more extreme, like a high stilton, a stilton from the beyond. (I joked about the expression 'dead hand'. Mine, half dead, must have courted Death in person. All you needed to do was give it a rub—like someone groping you up on the bus[9]). For days and days, as the newly aerated flesh began to change appearance, I went on avidly sniffing that lethal cocaine. It became a game, a tic. I feared the smell would finally evaporate, I sniffed a little more, and there it was: a sudden flash of flesh beyond flesh, the breeding ground of that spiraling putrefaction, an unnerving hint of fermented milk and curds, an aura of whey. And then the trail disappeared over the horizon of my skin-cell landscape.

Linked to this, there is the memory of a coat from the Caucasus.

Someone had bought it on some journey in some flea-market in some God-forsaken country on the Central Asian Steppe. Grey, stiff, feral, for a few days it must have looked fine on the streets of Moscow, but it was soon relegated to the back of a wardrobe. Months later, during a move, the owner starts to pack up his house. There's a terrible smell somewhere, and finally he finds the source. There it is, Lazarus-like, standing stiffly, riddled with worms, born again in a buzz of micro-organisms. The hide, tanned in a hurry, had come back to life (the exact opposite of my experience under the plaster cast). A splendid re-emersion, a powerful return from Hades, an imperious re-claiming of the senses in this coat of flesh. You could say that, while the coat was not dead enough, I was not alive enough. My wolf was there, crouching in my hands and howling.

Papilloma spreading through the organic tissue, epithelia of death.

XII

The skin, again

"Who can guarantee that people can actually see and hear? They are veritable beehives, such a crawling nest of parasites that one asks oneself if their bodies do not belong more to the worms than to themselves, and if, in the long run, they are nothing other than a kind of anthill." [10]

The skin, again, as a theatre of change. The treatment I used for my verucas—those repellent growths under the soles of your feet, nurtured by the humid atmosphere of swimming pools—was truly sensational. As if the agony of swimming lessons had not been enough of a punishment, the enemy was always ready to ambush you at that propitious moment when your bare foot involuntarily touched the marble floor of the pool. A month later the parasitic creature reared its ugly, phosphorescent-yellow head, like an extra-terrestrial monster. Normally you would need liquid azote, weapons from star wars, lasers, to root out the menacing colony of ultra-bodies, but I decided to do things my own way. I scraped the surface of my skin away, removed the nucleus of the colony, saturated the area with alcohol and set light to my foot. The city of Troy in flames. The operation left a dark crater, and in its ruins no form of life was ever to appear again.

The silent, devoted and gregarious dissemination of fungal skin infections were a different story. Soft, sub-glandular rings, chronic decay, peripatetic gangrene. When contaminated, the body produces foam, like waves frothing on the shore. The infection advances and retreats, with some areas of the body perennially affected by molecular vibration. I could call these areas borders of non-being, regions where corruption of the flesh represents a fundamental yet instable balance, and where the outlines of the organisms are blurred. They are atolls, a porous and mobile space where there is uninterrupted exchange between life and death. The tissue of certain infections is necrotic from the start, necrosis representing an outpost, a Consulate of Nothingness. Yet these *terrains vagues* are necessary—or, rather, homeopathically indispensable—for the regime of forces that govern us. Carpets of funguses, north-facing walls papered with lichen, are a sign that the Ego has already detached from the Id, and that it is ready to welcome these migrants, that it accepts making space for guests who have just arrived in a newly optimistic dawn of rottenness.

My right tympanum suffers endemic irritation, as do my feet, with the periodic erosion that goes by the name of athlete's foot. Equally endemic is the contamination of my extremities. They trade with the enemy, they weave matter with anti-matter, and moor the cytoplasm to the empty shore that surrounds it. Come to think of it, at the borders of the Empire, soldiers inevitably made contact with the Barbarians on the other side. And while I try different creams to halt the infection's progress, I fraternize with the enemy.

XIII

The holy foot

The pinnacles of the cathedral named Marie Reine-du-Monde and Saint-Jacques-le-Majeur (for Anglophone worshippers, Mary Queen of the World and Saint James the Greater) are suffocated by the surrounding skyscrapers. Don't let the double name deceive you: it's just a baby St Peter's.

The Bishop of Montréal went to Rome in 1870 to attend the Synod. He was so taken by the Basilica of St Peter's in the Vatican that he decided he would build a scale model as soon as he got back home. The church was finally consecrated in 1894. Here are some figures: 333 feet long, compared to the 730' of the original; 150' wide, compared to 262'; 252' high, compared to the nearly 500' of Michelangelo's dome. What has been changed? The ornamental statues on the facade do not represent the apostles but patron saints of the parishes in the province. What's missing? The piazza, the columned arcade, and the dome, which is taller and narrower than the original.

All this to say that the building is but the outward shell, the casing, the packaging of a deeper spatial disorientation that strikes a tourist from Rome. You walk into a church that feels familiar but to your amazement has somehow shrunk, as if you have grown and expanded inside like a seed in a pod. I've finally managed to fill the space! Remembering long childhood afternoons spent in those vertically challenging spaces, the phrase came to mind instinctively. While the replica of the Corinthian columned facade is impressive, the re-make of Bernini's bronze baldachin, made in Rome in 1900, is heart-breaking: the barley-sugar spiraled columns, twisting upwards towards the Christian heaven, the mystic hot-air balloon canopy is reduced to the dimensions of an economy car, a scalextric model, or electric train set.

A taste for hobby model building informs the interior of the church throughout. It looks like a construction set just out of its box, a light shade of green, lit by neon strips, sterile and hospital-like. The nuns look like nurses too. And at the end of the long ward lies the object of their medical attention: the foot of St Peter's statue.

Though it is the same size as the original, it has not been consumed, made smooth by kisses and caresses, as the equivalent has been in Rome. The bronze looks as though it has come straight out of the cast, still to be broken in by prayer. Oh come, all ye faithful, burnish it! Make it shine with tears and sighs—the same sighs that accompanied the crusade launched by Québec in support of the Papal States.

"Love God and go thy way". This was the motto of the five hundred and seven Pontifical Zouave volunteers that rushed to the defense of Rome against the invaders from the House of Savoy. The evidence is there for all to see: the regiment flags, uniforms, prayer books, and a painting of Colonel Athanase de Charette in the midst of battle. Piedmont soldiers depicted as Iroquois Native Americans. The sky heavy with snow, a tundra-like vegetation, the Canadian forces fight valiantly against the breach of the Aurelian walls at a Porta Pia-like gate which is projected onto a polar landscape. Our Risorgimento myth transformed into an arctic dream.

XIV

The whole episode could be summarized by a sound, the ping of a little stone. I had been waiting months for it (I knew the ping vibrating on a tuning fork would restore by body to its previous harmony). It heralded my freedom. Beware of falling rocks, road signs warn.

It all started one morning when I woke up with dagger-sharp stabs of pain in my stomach and back, but in the wrong direction, from inside to out. Kidney stones. Once this was clear, any residue of Titanic rebellion against my suffering soon evaporated. (As a child, in bed with flu, I always had my trusty, bright-red toy trumpet with me, ready to call for help, to call the world to witness my personal battle of the Roncevaux Pass[11]).

As if pain is not enough, there is also ridicule. I am ordered to keep my bladder filled, and to do so with religious discipline and zeal. Water as divine intervention. "Look at river meanders," the internist says. "Rivers don't get kidney stones." So I drink five, six, seven liters a day on an empty stomach. If I am travelling, for example, I always carry at least two bottles, the absolute minimum needed for the Great Urinary Decantation (the opposite of a diver with his oxygen tanks). There is also a spatial alteration in my body as the enormous volume of liquid in the cistern swings from side to side and echoes inside me. Whoosh, whoosh. I carry within me a water bag. I am an overflowing water bag. Or rather, it is as if, having made a river out of me, I am sitting on the bank and watching the violent effects of a sudden surge of rainwater. A wadi: heavy rain washing across a dry riverbed, filling the tanks and then draining away. All this in order to cleanse my hydraulic pipes, which are finally freed by that dry ricocheting shot, that little explosion, that ping of shiny crystal that comes out of my body, a home-made gold nugget.

XV

My kidney complications led to further ophthalmic trouble. At that time, in fact, I discovered my short-sightedness was getting worse. I went to a specialist, who confirmed my suspicions and went on to try and identify the possible causes. There was nothing obvious to start with, but then he interrogated me on my medical history and the story of the water came out.

The Story of the Water

The eye is a drum that stretches
under pressure. It is a frog trying to turn into an ox,
a hot air balloon, a rubber tire, a bagpipe.

Vision-bladder
The lenses of your glasses
are no barrier for the flow of your fluids
The banks will break, and when it spills over
the river of your gaze
will flush our stones and images
to widen your world.[12]

The result of the excessive liquid intake as a cure for my kidney stones was a stratum of gleaming, loamy deposit on the squamous bedrock of my cornea. Visual purple: rhodopsin. I imagined my gaze as the Nile, with its slow depositing of silt that I hoped would be beneficial, fertilizing the riverbed of my eye. The final situation was as follows: liters of water in one orifice, decompression eye-drops in another, in a delicate balancing act involving osmotic pressure, filters and communicating vessels. Death by Water. I was beginning to feel like Phlebas the Phoenician,[13] or like a Michelin man.

XVI

Tales on the theme of dilation (continued)

. . . the last time I asked myself such a question had to do with the cavity behind the knee. I remember a movie where it got talked about. Less than six months later, in that precise spot, I developed a cyst as big as a hunting rifle. That's when I discovered the cavity's name: the popliteal region. No sense operating, the cyst just grows back in a few years, like a lizard's tail. Disgusting metamorphosis. Of course I can no longer bend without difficulty.[14]

These notes should really be included in the section later on in the book on the so-called "cinematographic meniscus", but I think I need to deal with them now. During my convalescence after surgery on my left knee, I was persuaded to try out some ozone therapy. It's nothing to do with the hole in sky—at least I don't think so. I made an appointment in via Panama. The reason I mention the address is because during the whole session I had the constant sensation that my leg looked like the two American continents, the knee cap being the isthmus of Panama. At the same time, the pock-marked face of some Central American dictator appeared to flicker behind the stabs of pain. The locus of the operation, the area that needed attention, lay between the Mexican femur and Colombia (the head of the tibia). This is what happened.

First they inserted a needle into my synovial capsule (which seemed much tougher than normal, so they had to really work at it, as if they were trying to blow up one of those old leather footballs with a hand pump). Once they had found the right place, the next stage was to pump curative gas into the joint. That was when I was forced to watch my knee being transformed. It was like watching an animation in which the body changes, grows, swells up. What is more, and this was the most worrying part, emanating from the inner tube of my knee there was a clinking of ironware, nuts and bolts clanging, like the jingling of loose change in a pocket. By the end of the procedure my swollen leg began to lift upwards of its own accord. I couldn't look at the Zeppelin without getting anxious, so I asked them to stop. I'd had enough of Panama, enough of my knee. Now it just sits there in a corner.

XVII

For nearly fifteen years I had trouble with my tonsils. At the slightest provocation my glands would swell, and I would get a cough and a fever. And so it went on, right into full maturity, following an etiological pattern that was embarrassingly pubescent. I was like an air-bag. All was to be revealed when I got sick in France. In French I found out tonsils were called "amygdales".[15] Like flint arrow heads crafted by ancient populations, archeological finds from the Cenozoic era, these two pendants still dangle proudly in the exhibition space of my throat.

XVIII

The line to reach the glass cases moves slowly. A group of German tourists gets there first, and only when they have finished can you climb the stairs that lead to the heart of the basilica. This is not the only altar pilgrims head for. Judging by the numbers, in fact, it's not even the most popular (like a juke-box of desire, set off by pain rather than by small change). In the left nave, for example, a long queue waits patiently to go into the saint's vault. A cascade of votive offerings, a canopy of letters, photographs, drawings, covers the walls of the alcove, which is charged with religious fervor. The real center of the building, however, is in the fifth chapel of the ambulatory. This is the reliquary where what remains of St Anthony of Padua has come to rest.

Patron saint of travelers, earthquake victims, and thieves, of marriage, and of lost objects, his symbols include a book and a white lily. Among the exhumed body parts, St Anthony's shiny tongue is on show in an ostentatious gold and glass construction. A few years back, we heard on the news that the object had been abducted in order to extort money from the church. (How can you make your escape, in the dead of night, with a stolen tongue in your pocket as if it were a cigarette lighter which is so compact that it bounces in your pocket as you run? There will be no spark from that flintlock. There will be no words). Now the tongue is back in its rightful place: gloomy, petrified blood. Ready to emanate its grim energy as if it were an atomic nucleus, a tablet of uranium in a submarine-sanctuary, towers and pinnacles like periscopes, cupolas like portholes, for seven centuries of navigation.

It's no ordinary tongue, however sacred. It's the tongue of the great preacher. And yet, strange though it may seem, though the relic is much loved it fades in comparison with what is beside it. The case is less known, its contents less shocking, but more abstract, abstruse, and incongruous. The vocal apparatus of the saint, all of its essential parts faithfully reconstructed. Imagine a constellation, a pattern of tiny bones and cartilage placed carefully on crystal glass blocks. A reproduction of St Anthony's laryngeal system in perfect spatial equilibrium. A wind gallery where there is no wind, and where there never will be again. We see a voice. Or rather, we see the source of the phonation that gave voice to one of the greatest church orators. A monument to the memory of sound. But it is like seeing a voltaic arc without its spark, or a computer without an operating program. Perhaps the value of a body is precisely this transient capacity to "execute a program" for an individual. But not for long. The voice, the soul, is the software that is needed to run it.

XIX

While on the subject, I must tell you about the afternoon I spent at home after a heart check up. It appeared that I had a heart murmur. Just like that, a bolt out of the blue. My inner tube was punctured. I was upset by this new development, but, luckily, the diagnosis turned out to be wrong. The effect on me, however, was that for the umpteenth time I felt my body was irredeemably unreliable. It was the same shadow line, I now realize, as the one I would develop with regard to computers. Defenseless against their failures. Vulnerable and technopathic.

Often their failures depend on the electricity grid. The most common problem is known as 'sag', that is, when there is a temporary reduction in electricity supply. The cause of this reduction (as if blood stopped flowing into the brain) is attributable to a sudden request for energy in order to run too many machines at the same time (engines, compressors, elevators). Hiccups (or murmurs) of this kind create havoc with modems, printers, serial ports, plotters, answering machines and light bulbs.

As a counterpoint to these sags, there can also be sudden vertiginous increases in power, lasting mere milliseconds, known as 'spikes'. These are normally the result of the electricity coming back after a black out, and they propagate along the grid like hurricanes, laying waste to everything on their path. Yet another phenomenon is the 'surge', an increase in supply similar to a spike but lasting longer (up to a twentieth of a second). These three types of excessive oscillation stress out electronic components, and lead to their untimely death. And that's without even mentioning viruses and other contagious bacteria that inhabit the cybernetic lazaret—that wretched tangle that inspires the same distrust I feel towards my own organism, sags, spikes and surges coursing through its wiring, burning neurons, creating blockages.

(More on the dynamics of the heart murmur. A whisper of air. A guest who met his death because of a faulty heater, having dined with me no more than two days before. Silent but smiling. When the smile was gone, the silence remained—but the presence of the smile transformed the consistency of the silence. Dinner companion, dispatch rider, relay racer. He had survived 40 years, long enough to meet me. Is it possible that his mission was just that? To inhabit me and then vanish? At least with butterflies there's coupling. A coupling of smiles? My egocentrism, my centripetalism. Or a murmur and then nothing. A whisper of air that touches him, then nothing. A pneuma, a punctured pneumatic tire. As if the smile were an effect of a loss. He wasn't smiling, or waving goodbye. As he left, his spirit rippled his lips. Clothes hanging on the line blowing in the wind.)

XX

On the field hospital Philip II of Spain installed in the Basilica of El Escorial.

Jamais vieux Pharaon, au flanc d'un mont d'Egypte
Ne fit pour sa mourire une plus noire crypte.[16]

Lattice-work, a transistor, a microchip, a psycho-chip replicated everywhere. A representation of St. Lawrence's *parilla*, the gridiron on which he was said to have been martyred. This almost commercial logo, which corresponds to the floor plan of the Escorial, is obsessively reproduced in souvenirs and on the walls of restaurants. Even on the headboard of my bed. But what a surprise to find the Basilica at the center of the gridiron pattern and, at the center of the Basilica, the royal chapel.

Philip II had it built ten or so meters to the right of the main altar, openly inspired by St. Peter's in Rome. Imagine! My nightmare as a child was the idea of having to sleep the night in those empty naves. But Philip chose to do so. Chateaubriand in Westminster Cathedral, Belfagor in the Louvre: rather like being locked in school when classes are over. A buried sovereign. A hypogeum. You can keep an eye on the *ostensorium*[17] from your stone pillow.

Philip II lies watching the Divine Mover. He's in a tomb. He's Montezuma. No, he's Tutankhamun at the heart of his pyramid. As if he were resting in the tabernacle, camping out close to God. At night!

Celestial radio-transmitter, theological emissions. The priest-king's presence is pervasive, asymmetric. He is the worm in the apple. He lies watching the seed, to his left. God's parasite. Its sleeping place. El Escorial a cocoon for the maggot-king.

The king next to the altar is God's thorn in the flesh (the thorn has pierced almost to the heart) . A blood-clot, or, again, a spear in the ribs. Royal, ventricular sacrilege. Escorial = scoria or scum (It must mean something that this is the only library in the world where books are shelved with their bindings inwards. Is it to preserve them better, as they claim, or is it to hide their titles, their names, their *principium individuationis*?[18]).

What if all this were simply an oxygen tent, set up in order to perform a by-pass operation on the divinity's heart? "The patient has received a valve which is now able to regulate the cardiac system." The operating theater: "urgent request for surgery". And the divinity allows himself to be operated on, indeed gives his permission.

This King lives in a church. A divine shack. But he is also a king-butler, a king-bodyguard (the royal soldiers keep vigil outside his lordship's room). It is a desperately arrogant and mad attempt to integrate and ingratiate himself. (Like the joke about Christ ascending to heaven with a centurion holding onto his ankles wanting to go with him. When Jesus notices, he kicks him away, saying he's off to the house of his Father. Here the King is playing the part of the centurion, and God will be sure to shake him off; one day he will be free of him!).

The clandestine King. Stowed away illegally in the ship's hold.

Or, finally, the King is part of an expedition towards God, the advance party. His bed represents the base-camp before the final ascension. His high-altitude bivouac is a last refuge, a place to contemplate the final mountain climb. The Sherpas chat quietly around the campfire, and he contemplates, dreams, gazes at the horizon, and prays before scaling the Grade 6 face of divinity.

A corollary of sorts

A few miles away, there's the massive stone monument carved into the rocks by General Franco in the Valley of the Fallen. I discovered two unverified facts there:

1. Francisco Franco kept St Teresa's arm on his bedside table;
2. Roughly thirty years ago, an arm of St Teresa (the same one?) was taken around every village in Spain in a glass case shaped like an elbow.

I'm attracted by this viral idea of reliquaries, by the fact that they are taken around in order to spread salvation. A dead limb on tour.

XXI

Arm, hand, writing. Might we consider our handwriting our personal halo? After all, this is a part of our body too. German lessons in Brema, the city of fabled musicians in the North of the country. Musical boredom, following the melody of an infinite plateau of a long afternoon. And suddenly a blackboard confession. This was where I was shocked to find that the simple gesture of exposing your handwriting in public required a great deal of courage.

As the teacher picked up the chalk to write something I felt bad for him. I felt bad because—although the act is purely mechanical—we reveal the most intimate details about ourselves on a blackboard. The genitalia, the shamefulness of the sign. The pornography of an autograph. Behind the stutter there was a deformed scrawl.

It reminds me of that film in which the heroine betrays her husband. Folded into the arms of her lover, standing in a field, she sees a plane writing words in the sky. She looks at the trail of smoke and cries, "It's not him, that's not his handwriting!"

I think of that scene, an ideal continuation of *Mrs. Dalloway*[19], every time I struggle with my notes. A knot of inextricable and inexplicable lines, a tangled skein of silk, the scribbling of a madman. When I read my notebooks I have to decipher myself; that is, I have to unravel the threads of my writing, the knot tightened by haste and annoyance. It makes me wonder whether our handwriting changes when we are ill, and, if it does, in what way the illness insinuates itself into its form. Whether it contaminates the curve, or tightens the knot.

Every sign hampers progress, as if the marks on the page were figures in disguise. What did that 'r' mean? Who was that 'r' referring to? Or maybe it wasn't an 'r' after all. But it's too late. The meaning has already vanished because the handwriting takes off, and as it flies away it takes with it whatever significance it had once expressed. Forever. No secret service will ever be able to break the code.

(On the side. Years and years of studying and I have hardly anything to show for it. I ask myself, is there such a thing as linguistic insufficiency in the same way as there is, say, liver insufficiency? I think there must be. My German, for example, is a rickety creature. I can tell as soon as I have to speak to somebody. The scrawny fellow has been sitting there for twenty years, wizened and bent—double in a corner, a shrunken beggar unable to stir. If you call him, he struggles to get up, barely nods, and looks away. Things weren't much better at the beginning to tell the truth. I remember how discouraged I got when I mixed up *aufsatz* with *aussatz.*[20] Just one consonant different and chaos suddenly and implausibly takes over.

XXII

Paris. Treasures of the French language. An exhibition of 393 original documents, manuscripts, hand corrected galley proofs, first editions. The show opens with an ancient vellum, the *Serments de Strasbourg* penned in the year 842 in a dialect more Latin than anything else. In another piece, the *Séquence de Sainte Eulalie*, you are witness to the birth of a new animal species, tiny creatures swarming over the pages, destined to multiply into an organism of remarkable complexity. Like embryos or germs on a petri dish, the twenty nine bacterial lines of the prayer are a breeding ground for the millennial development of poetry.

Walking through the exhibition you encounter travel diaries, medieval collections, typographic manuals, drawings, letters, maps, medical and architectural tracts. André Chanier's prison poems[21] scribbled in minuscule notebooks later to be smuggled out with the laundry are emotionally charged. A kind of writer's Tom Thumb, leaving crumbs behind unbeknownst to his executioner. Except in this story, there is a tragic ending: the protagonist is sent to the guillotine. The writer is dead, but his handwriting is still here, heightening the vaguely mournful atmosphere of these rooms, filled with funereal stationary: quills, pencils, ink wells, hand casts and death masks. Tomb treasures. Instead of mummies, there are these papers densely filled with history, an ossuary of handwritten words.

XXIII

Paris again. The monumental cemetery. The gigantic necropolis, built on the same city plan as the French capital, is a network of streets and squares divided into *avenues, chemins, carrefours and arrondissements.*[22] A city of the dead, built in a spirit that was both monumental and neighborly, celebratory and constructive. Forty-four hectares,[23] of which more than a fifth designated as 'romantic' areas, twelve thousand trees, a hundred thousand tombs and a million burials, the most famous of which are advertised in the guide books, where the dead are classified by name and profession, in alphabetical order.

Reading from publicity material I pick up at the main gate: "Inaugurated by Napoleon in 1804, the Père Lachaise cemetery has been a theatre for a highly original initiative. In order to valorize the area, the administration has organized the rental of electric golf carts for members of the public. The tours will be announced in the newspapers and on the computerized Minitel network: code OFFI, number 3615, initials VG. The 2 person vehicles can be hired for a minimum of one hour."

With very little expense, a map of the cemetery in hand, I am currently making my way silently and rapidly down an avenue on a scooter. The sun is shining coldly in the bright blue sky. I am the only motorized client of the administration, and apart from a roadblock caused by a group of admirers of Yves Montand[24] (who died just yesterday), there are no driving problems whatsoever. I've already worked out where I'm going: on a Vespa to Hades.[25] Shivering behind me, my friend is somewhat disconcerted. I'm driving (and the windscreen decorations, with Greek fret patterns, billow like flags at half-mast). I'm well equipped, with gloves and a scarf, while he is breathing heavily, unconvinced. He doesn't even have a driver's license. Driving the scooter in this mortuary miniature of the Ville Lumière[26], I feel as though I'm forming a new attitude to death. A touristic, drive-by experience—neither blasphemous nor ironic, but certainly panoramic.

XXIV

A quick change of scene. A motor racing circuit, high speed engines revving towards you and then revving away again. I know these provincial tracks well: hay bales, pilots with exotic names (like Moreno), the smell of exhaust fumes, threatening glares, spilt oil, the atmosphere of a country fair. It was in a place like this that I got lost for the first time as a young child. I wandered around in the middle of the oval, a solar system of go-karts whizzing at full speed around me. I was circling too, without knowing why, at the center of an armillary sphere of ear-splitting noise, the rings of the astrolabe increasingly out of sync. I don't think I ever recovered from this experience, though in the end my grandparents found me on the edge of a curve designed to look like the parabola at Monza.

I can't imagine anything more depressing than a car race. I was confirmed in this view a few years later when I had to have a check-up for problems with my circulation. The procedure wasn't painful, except for the fact that I had to wait for hours (I always read while I'm waiting, and have developed an immense store of paramedical knowledge over decades spent in doctors' waiting rooms). They stuck a set of wires up my leg and then attached them to two boxes that looked like stereo speakers. Sitting at the console, the doctor turned up the volume, set up the synthesizer and connected up with the system. I was ready for the usual hi-fi consultation, but then I heard an indistinct crackle. The noise got louder and slowly a line took shape on the screen, a representation of sound, not yet a tune. Then came the unmistakable noise.

I recognized it at once. It was the voice of the racing car approaching the grandstand then vanishing. Spikes and dips, asymmetrically penned on the sonogram. I am thrown back into the circuit, cars wailing around me: it is my own blood circulating in the race track of my veins and arteries, pulsating, pushing, passing. The Doppler effect. I realize that the melancholy memory is a representation of my being. My existence is itself a circuit. Inside my body an interminable and obsessive Indianapolis Grand Prix is taking place. Even more, my body is nothing more than a trial circuit, and the molecules that make it up are both formally and consubstantially out of tune. You never think about it, but blood plasma, with its globules and platelets, runs all the time. It hurls itself along the track, takes pit stops for gas and repairs, then races back to the competition. And I don't need to take a step. All I need to do is sit in the grandstand, an anxious spectator at the Cardiac Grand Prix.

XXV

A propos of blood running…

. . . when the evening news sounds like a Greek Tragedy. An earthquake in the region of Naples. In the middle of the night, roused by the noise, a father wakes up and runs to his son's bedroom. The walls and the floor are moving, the lamps are swinging, the furniture is creaking, in the drawers the cutlery is rattling, teaspoons touching spoons, high on the shelves the grappa glasses are tinkling, in its bottle the scarlet Archimes liqueur is rolling in waves that are too small to be measured on the Beaufort scale—with all this going on around him the man rushes into the bedroom of his son and finds him bleeding out on the floor. The boy had chosen that very night to commit suicide.

So, I wonder, what invisible thread connected the oscillations of the earthquake with those of the heart? What made the blood run that night? What rumbling cataclysm conflated something so big with something so small? Havoc on earth with the miserable blood-letting of the boy? The seismic event in the veins of the son, the earthquake in the veins of the father, leave the two protagonists immobilized in my memory. Pillars of salt. There is no second act in this Tragedy.

XXVI

Let me go back to those electric wires. A couple of weeks after my first sonogram, I was subjected to a brilliant variation of the Doppler. Slap-stick comedy, more like. Laurel and Hardy-like gags that left us all in fits of giggles. The technical term for the procedure is electromyography, but it felt more like a puppet show as I myself was transformed into a marionette—without the pedigree of Kleist's dialogue "On the Marionette Theater"[27]. Electrodes again, more wires, more special effects. I was invited to lie on the doctor's table. The show began at low voltage.

Small shocks to start with, in order to evaluate the electronic activity of my leg muscles. Then the intensity, and pain, increases. Every time the electric current is switched on, my leg jumps of its own accord. Totally of its own accord. I have nothing to do with it. It lifts itself independently of me and that is what's so strange. An epileptic Punch, his head down on his left shoulder in order to grab the stick that's going to beat Judy. A twitch, a jerk, like an orgasm, the motions of sexual possession. These strange spasms are the infallible proof that our body responds to external forces. When it is merely a vehicle of an alien force—be it the voice of the dead or of the gods (or both, perhaps, when we are having sex)—when, that is, a human being is emptied and the hand that holds it guides its movements, the limbs move randomly. The body is a live wire off a grid that leaps out of your hands, or a water pump too powerful to hold.

The comedy of the performance depended on the complete independence of one element from the rest, and, more importantly, from what is supposed to be the generating station for my impulses. Thus, with regard to my leg, my body is "other", and the leg keeps jerking without the central nervous system being able to do anything about it. Off you go, leg! Ah, there you are, Mr. Leg! A character in a Gogol novel. The mad doctor increases the doses of electricity, triggering the secession of the leg, which starts dancing a Neapolitan *saltarello*, a dance of Saint Vitus.[28]

I'm a top, a screw
Coming unscrewed.[29]

I've always been morbidly afraid of the idea that the unity of my organism could come under threat. This is why I'm so horrified by torture. As it is, cutting nails or hair, defecating even, requires saying goodbye to a part of your body. An excremental interpretation of matter triumphs in my mind. According to this concept, every nail, every hair is also God's: or, as Joubert put it, "spirit (pure spirit)" as opposed to matter, which is excess (*excrementum* or what is rejected). This matter, he continues, using a rather coarse image, is "the effect of digestion, the residue of its immortal food which is thought."[30]

What I am saying is that the secession of one part of the body from the whole is a precursor of future disassembly—a *memento mori*. Remember, you are destined to die, remember your leg is not yours. Just look if you don't believe it! It's dancing away on its own, hanging from the strings of the electric puppeteer. Now it's back again. The same leg, the one with the floating knee. I'll treat it well now that we're back together again. Who knows? It might not be for that long.

XXVII

By contrast, I have no idea what illness to connect the next story to. I am in the latency phase. An important detail to bear in mind: I'm in short pants. Somebody takes me to the barber's, or rather, drops me off at the barber's. It's the difference between these two verbs that dictates the symptomology of this case. They say they'll come and pick me up. If this is true, who's coming? And when? I'm getting a nasty feeling that I'm 'missing in action', since my hair has been shorn off at least an hour ago and there's no rescue brigade at the door. After kicking around in the store for a while, I stand behind the glass door and stare out at the street. This is when the cramp comes.

I don't know what caused these intestinal spasms. I suffer in silence, and words stick in my throat. I can't utter a sound, I can't even lift a finger to attract someone's attention or ask for help. In paralyzed silence I stare outside. In paralyzed silence I melt; the product of my body slides down my leg, slowly at first, then uncontrollably. I am turned into a little abdominal candle consecrated to the patron saint of deserters. That is what I feel like as the fecal matter slips further down my leg—little migratory birds? Reptiles? A votive offering?

Later on in life I read these enchanting words about excrement, guts and rear ends. Ontological metabolism.

If you want to you can discover the truth
Even in the backside, even in the behind.
Only look backwards
To see how the candle of death burns eternally,
Fuelled by the fat of yourself,
Burning you like pine pitch
Melting you, bone and marrow,
Like butter in the sun.[31]

I can still see myself exposed behind the glass, turned inside out by the stares of the passers-by, a sea-cucumber of myself, my soft intestine losing or emitting that sickly paste. A black teardrop with no mourning (a comet, a lethal mushroom, a giant pod). A counter-me, a walking shadow, a living, self-propelled thing moving down my rigid corpse. I was making space in the afterworld.

XXVIII

I promise I will not write about what Edmund Spenser called "egestions of the Port of Esquiline".[32] There's no need to indulge, as the significance of the release from oneself afforded by breaking wind is only too clear. There are other more disturbing forms of *Aufhebung*[33]that need exploring. For example, the inconceivable discomfort you feel after a fight when your nose has shifted position. Yes, that's what I said: when your nose is no longer where you left it. You look at yourself in the mirror appalled and can't believe your eyes. Where's it gone? Where have I gone? The face is no longer mine. You feel as if your body is about to fall apart, like a pack of cards thrown into disarray by the wind.

Well, in this regard I can still remember the panic I felt when the cat I used to play with as a child got stuck and then freed himself. I don't know which little bone, his scapula perhaps, gave way. The worst part was that there was no apparent pain. He simply came out crooked, and adjusted naturally to this unexpected shape, inhabiting his new body with ease. As I watched with horror, he gave himself a good shake and the domino pieces fell back into place once again. I never touched him again.

Remember, your body is a Rubik's cube. At the moment all your parts may have fallen into the right combination, but all you need to do is shift things a bit and you're in trouble!

XXIX

I still remember the shame I felt as a teenager about my armpits. I couldn't accept them. I couldn't accept that my pre-pubescent arms were gone forever. They had once been light and thin, porous and resistant, like the pelican bones described by D'Annunzio[34], "lighter than blown glass, lighter than laminated aluminum." The light metal alloy that had made my arms fragile and fluorescent as neon tubes had been replaced by hefty, heavily articulated body mass. The force of gravity exerted its *droit du seigneur*. My body became a bundle of integument, muscle and skin that would inevitably rot. My task in the years to come was to find the courage and the capacity to transform myself into what I had already become.

Many years later, standing in front of a store window, I look up and see a man staring at me. It's me again. The light cruelly cuts off the curve of my forehead and reveals a new shiny patch of skin. It takes a while for my nauseated eyes to adjust as I swallow yet another dose of unfamiliar baldness. Humiliating negotiations of this kind, however, pale in comparison to the far more painful double reflection.

We are so used to the infinite compromises we make with our appearance that we are unprepared for witnessing it from both sides. When this image ambushes us as we walk between two mirrors (say at the barber's, or when trying on some clothes), our disgust has no limits. Years of patient self-acceptance are swept away by the irredeemable physical imperfections and imbalances on view. When right and left are reinstated, the epiphany of our orthogonal identity is inescapable. Our habit of mentally erasing a curve on one side and accentuating it on the other—the well-meaning art of compensation—makes the axis of our face careen dangerously to one side. Once the mask is lifted, our true identity is revealed, turned inside out by the false image like a caricature. The line of vision is inverted, the vessel veers to one side, the rudder is off route, the nose is off center. Set off balance by this unexpected spray, the inexorable wind doesn't give us time to redistribute our weight, move things around, re-align the keel of our face, and we capsize.

Askew, awry, with a receding hairline, my ego looks at myself.

XXX

I once read that "health is life lived in the silence of the organs."[35] That's all very well, but there's a veritable bacchanalia going on in my body. Cartilage creaking, pieces rattling like coins in the collection bag shaken by the priest up and down the pews for Sunday donations. Maybe that's what my body's doing: begging for alms? Is the poor creature ready to be made into an *ex voto*?

XXXI

Somewhere inside me resides the enigmatic figure of Tycho Brahe[36]. His name sounds like that of a precision watch and is enough on its own to grab my attention. But his life…studying the stars in the sixteenth century, the sword duel in which he lost part of his nose, the precious silver replacement. His name is his prosthesis. The two things are one: a thing which is silver and ticks. An arrow head, a clock hand. A clock-man. To add to my fascination—as if all this were not enough—there was his death by water. Unwilling to get up from the banquet table so as not to upset the King, Tycho controlled his bladder to the extent that later he was unable to relieve himself. A body unable to rebel against the social body. Tycho died because he could not piss, and ever since then tourists visiting the castle in Prague have taken the piss. A grotesque example of martyrdom to etiquette, but, I can't help admiring the man. Bent double at the King's court, his face fashionably painted, holding out until he collapsed, wracked by his body fluid. There it is again: the revenge of the organism against the ecliptic path of the sun and other celestial calculations.

XXXII

I was always told not to pick my nose, "or it would turn into a cave for sheep to sleep in." Of course the result of these threats was that I saw my body as a vast, uninhabited area like the Sardinian Barbagia[37]. What else was I supposed to think, when I convince myself that every orifice of my body is inhabited—or, worse, could be inhabited—by an animal, or a hostage? Think about your belly-button. It starts out as a lead for the fetus orbiting in celestial-maternal, ethereal-uterine space. It ends up as a hurried knot, to remind us that we are no more than fair balloons that have been inflated and then twisted and tied into different shapes.

XXXIII

Looking over old Jerusalem from the car park on the Mount of Olives (yes, there's a car park on the Mount of Olives…), the city spreads out before your eyes in all its chaotic glory—layers of dazzling history, a golden construction site. We are on one ridge and Jerusalem is on another. Between us a rift: the Valley of Josaphat, not just any old valley. According to the prophet Zechariah, this is where the Last Judgment would take place. Just behind the car park. We don't even need to get out of the car.

Even though it's a really nice day, our guide suggests we stay where we are, while rummaging between the seats of the Fiat. Shall we get out? No, he answers. The inside of the car is starting to heat up, and he's playing with paper and scissors. He cuts out two large letter Ls, turns one upside down and fits them together. They represent the land of Israel, he says, as the Fiat 127 becomes uncomfortably hot. He sticks them on the windscreen against the light and slightly shifts the two letters so that the Ls are no longer touching, the space that has been opened up between them the light of the sky. The square is the Dead Sea, he explains, and the crack he has opened is the River Jordan (it's a zigzag, like the number 7 you make when you rip a jacket).

Thanks to these scraps of paper I learned about the geological breach that took place in the Middle East many millennia past. In a southerly direction, towards the African Great Lakes, a massive cataclasis gradually formed a rift, shifting African and Asian tectonic plates. I hold up the two cut-outs and try and imagine a tear going all the way down to the dark continent. Mr. Scissor Hands nods, and finally gestures to us that we can get out of the car.

We come out onto the Temple Mount, in front of the Dome of the Rock where Jewish tradition claims an angel stopped Abraham from sacrificing Isaac, where it is believed King Solomon lay the cornerstone of the first temple, where the prophet Mohammed allegedly ascended into heaven on his white horse. The shrine englobes the Mount Moriah ridge, and in the interior the naked, totemic foundation stones are protected by a circular wall. Circumcised. A thousand square feet or so, a decent sized apartment. And yet this was the launching pad for convulsive celestial comings and goings.

Intense air traffic with angels landing, prophets taking off, ascensions, and assumptions; a ganglion of spiritual energy.

I wander around the Dome. The only place I can't go and see is a tiny side door. A custodian bars my way. A gaggle of women in black veils are allowed through, but I am not. A French guy gets the go ahead, but I do not. I give up. I ask my friend whether I'm missing something important. No, he says. Are you sure? I insist. He reassures me: there's a dark, smelly burrow, that's all. But I am not satisfied and can't help asking one more question, which turns out to be fatal—a stab in the heart. "Well, does this burrow at least have a name?" My friend sighs, and with what little patience he has left, tries to fend off my enquiries. "A name? Not really… you could call it a nickname."

In one breath (the desperate breath of the tourist-collector, lost in a sea of shadows that only the complete series, or rather the completeness of the series, can dissipate—a traveler who studies his guidebook, chooses what to see, goes to see the sights he has selected, then erases them forever from his list of sights to see in the future, feels relieved of his duty, relieved to have fulfilled his duty, and can finally rejoice in the knowledge that he has "seen" and is "free to see no more."), in one breath, I was saying, I ask, "and what is this nickname?" My friend answers: "they call it the Navel of the World."

Silence. The navel of regret. What umbilical cord has been severed? From what belly-button have I been excluded? In the Holy Land, in this Land of the Hole cut by scissors, who has decided to cut me off?

XXXIV

I admit I neglected my back until I was at least thirty. It kindly reminded me of its existence one bright day in July. I was bending down, minding my own business, when suddenly a blinding bolt of lightning galvanized me from behind, the electricity darting down from my neck, attentively enveloping me. The power instantly pooled in my lower back, its magic mantle flashing glorious white light. The flash was my back's way of announcing I had thrown it out completely—what some people call a witch's blow.[38] This turn of phrase which evokes liqueur and chocolates cannot fail to render the polyphonic beauty of the piece I was about to play.

(I tend to see pain or illness as a composition to be performed differently every time. Every interpretation is new but the music never changes.)

Back to the back-ache. André Breton, writing about Picasso, said that everything the artist did was physiological[39]—even the way he piled up packets of cigarettes to look like a spinal column. It's these packets of cigarettes that are causing me pain, two of them in particular. The pain is not the result of a defect in the vertebrae, however. It is caused by the way they are put together. The pain, one could say, stems from their distance or, rather, their excessive proximity. Two parts touch, creating attrition. And the train comes to a halt:

I was approaching with blocked wheels
Contracted vertebrae
Hyphenated-words[40]

The reason the train metaphor came to mind is that, later on, I was pulled like a railcar by a locomotive into the tunnel of a CT scan and showered with garishly colored radiation. Two metal screws were in plain sight, the rivets in the cavity of the *os coxae* evidence that I was definitively screwed (in the shadowy X-ray, the titanium bed-knob of the hip replacement shone like a light from the depths of the hip bone). Since then, bit by bit, I've regained my flexibility, but I am condemned to a life-sentence of exercises.

There are no words to describe the boredom of this daily practice. It brings me back to my swimming days when I counted lengths mechanically, like an accountant. Like a blind-folded child back in the days of black and white television extracting the winning lottery numbers one by one.

I find myself lying on my back in hotel suites and cheap motel rooms, at friends' houses, in tents, railroad cars, guest houses, parking lots (I only need a few square feet), desperately trying to pull the same four vertebrae up like a rolling shutter, to make space, freshen up, let the sun in. I would like calisthenics to be subtracted from the final sum of my life, together with all the other tiresome daily tasks required of us—like flossing—in order to stay shipshape. People ask why I don't want a dog in the house… I already have one, devouring my time and pissing on it too. (Outside the room where I am doing my exercises you can hear my groans, or, when things are going well, the murmur of a short prayer offered to the disjointed God of this calcined bone-Lego creature).

XXXV

Giacomettiana

Giacometti[41] wanted to be lopsided. When he was involved in a car accident, his wish came true—he was left with a permanent limp. There's another element of his biography, however, that always struck me, and it started at around the same time as the accident. I think it was actually his new-found invalidity that helped the artist solve his problem, a problem I could ascribe to the terrible family of conditions I would call "vanishing figurines".

Whatever Giacometti touched would disappear, miniscule figures got smaller and smaller, more and more distant. Where did they go? Nothingness took them over. Day by day Giacometti's sculptures would shrink further: "In 1940, much to my terror, the statues started to get smaller. It was a dreadful catastrophe [...]. They became so small that I could no longer give them any features."[42]

His mother, greatly disturbed, confessed she was horrified by these miniature people and scolded him for making them. But he carried on, however shakily.[43] He could do nothing about the mutations. Dismayed and appalled, Giacometti wrote: "I didn't understand what was going on. All my statues ended up no more than a centimeter tall. One push and whoops! No more statue."[44]

The figurines became more and more diminutive, a limit of a sequence of integers, a mathematical dive. When, in 1945, Giacometti left Geneva, they all fit into a matchbox ("little burnt funereal steles, but this is to speak of the flame"[45]). I can imagine the rattling sound they made in his pocket, loose change. Morse Code. *Mors Tua.*

In the end the blood-letting was stemmed and the emptiness filled. In the end his space-ship managed to get out of the black hole (I see him as a tormented, wiser, older version of Dr Spock in *Star Trek*, with his ears sticking out as a result of his obsessive practice of listening). In the end Giacometti was able to exclaim: "I've sworn to myself never to allow my statues to shrink to an inch."[46] But what a price! So many figurines swallowed up by the vacuum! So many sculptures on death row!

Osiris in the Louvre: funereal, Egyptian, worn by time and darkness. This kind of art is for the dead, for those who continued to grab all the available space, like a couple fighting over the covers in a double bed.

XXXVI

It was summer in the city, and we were having dinner *al fresco*. I had parked the car close to the restaurant, in a wide open piazza that sloped downhill like an amphitheater. We ate heartily and drank heavily, without a care in the world. In fact I remember nothing about the evening except that it was pure, full, replete—and thereby empty of me. A vacation from my ever-looming awareness. Usually I weigh upon myself, I am my own promontory, always present and mindful of myself, always on the cliff-edge, always over the top. But that evening I was happy. A guardian asleep on the job.

Later, when I get up from the table, I go back to the car which is parked nearby. The night is warm, there has been wine. I turn the ignition, get into gear and then start daydreaming. Not for long. Rousing myself, suddenly back to my senses, I grab the wheel and push my foot down on the brake. To no avail. I realize that the car is moving of its own accord. Moments of terror and glory. Like a toy pulled by a blue cord, my little tin box inches slowly forwards—have you ever seen the toy soldier sitting in the driver's seat manage to direct the child who is doing the pulling?

Just a few yards of bewilderment and liberation. All I could do was watch. And I watched the mellow trajectory made by my docile car with me sitting docilely inside it: a perfect arc like the two-handed verónica of an exhausted torero's cape.[47] That is, until the hood of the car, having traversed the whole square, crashed into a line of garbage cans, where my golden arrow finally came to a halt.

Still in pain from the impact, I sat in the car contemplating the beauty of the astral semi-circle created by the piazza. That was when I discovered that the brakes and steering wheel were blocked by an anti-theft car-lock I had bought that same evening. I had forgotten to take it off. Now I knew what had tied me to an invisible external axis (the leg of a compass? Hamlet's Mill[48]?); my center was lying outside myself.

XXXVII

Partial paralyses, latent, looming, rheumatism, imminent arthritis. Time insinuates itself in the guise of alteration:

For a voice does grow old,
even in sound is the bone of time
even in the breath..[49]

My father told me he had once been enrolled in medical school. He went to classes for a couple of months until one morning he had to witness an operation. On the table was a woman with arthritis, her fingers, hands and feet as curved and gnarled as branches. With some elegance they pruned her tree. My father fainted, was taken out of the operating theatre, and became an engineer.

This anecdote comes to mind every time I feel a piece of cartilage is getting thicker, or whenever my left shoulder clicks against its joint before I go to sleep (like a railroad switch for sleep, sending the car to a dead-end track), or my heartbeat goes up. The Crooked Lady comes to mind because the first stirrings of death are in our joints, in our seized-up intersections, in the soft circumvolutions of our brain cells. We die on a curve, where it gets harder to move, where we need to make circular movements with our limbs, where we need to shift our way of thinking a few degrees one way or another. We die of rust and tartar, we die of erosion and earwax; like ruins we are grown over by a molecular jungle.

Rheumatic Concomitant Causes

Listen! It's late. I live in an apartment on the beltway I call "the Puddle". I would say ninety percent of my intellectual activity is absorbed by registering the sounds of honking, braking and shouting outside. Rather like those images showing the functional connectivity of your cerebral cortex which are almost entirely occupied by the shape of an over-sized thumb—the contrastive tomography requiring more energy than that needed to found an entire civilization.

The house breathed, it hyper-ventilated. My father used to call the gap between the window and its frame a 'walnut' because you could push one through without cracking the shell or crushing the kernel. We had a lot of 'walnuts' in the apartment. I picture myself striking a heroic pose, like those portraits of the young Napoleon on his skittish horse explaining battle strategy to his soldiers, an unruly tuft of hair lifted by the wind. In my case, my locks would fly on any day in November, even with the windows closed.

The decision was made to call a workman to laminate the window-frames. It was the first time I had met this figure, though he was evidently well acquainted with the inhabitants of the "Puddle". He came to the house with a tin barrel filled with silvery, scintillating, sonorous strips of steel—Apollo's quiver. He pulled out a drill and set to work. For a small sum, he nailed the strips onto the windows obliquely so that when they closed they fit the frame perfectly. No more 'walnuts'. A half-day's work and I was able to sleep in relative silence, hermetically sealed.

I'm in a vacuum. It's a strange sensation, an unreal, sweet holding of breath. I'm like Pipìn the free-diver,[50] immune to waves from the outside, locked in my time aquarium. I was truly happy for at least two days. A sound-proofed, underwater existence, somewhat dull, somewhat enclosed. And then there was this smell, a little high, a stench of damp...

That was when I lifted my gaze and saw that the ceiling had grown a green lawn. Mold. Lovingly cultivated mold. Under the mattress colonies of fungi and lichen were expanding. The laminator was called back and for the same sum was asked to dismantle everything. That is why I am now writing with difficulty, sheets of paper flying. The windows are closed but the breeze pushes my pen and a shiver goes up my spine.

XXXVIII

In the Summer of 1974, I spent two months in a hospital after a car accident. I lay flat on my back, immobilized, a pin through my tibia. The steel wire sticking out of my leg hung from a pulley a few feet over the bed, in its turn regulated by a system of lead weights. A scale model of a cable car—whose function was to place the femur in traction and thus to mend the fractured pelvis.

When they hammered in the knee pin I was given epidural analgesia—a form of anesthetic openly inspired by Socrates's experience with hemlock (the poison is travelling, can you still feel your legs?). My neighbor, in the operating theater straight after me, was not so lucky. I followed the barbaric procedure inflicted on this patient with horror, one doctor approaching him with a Black and Decker drill in his hand, hidden in a newspaper, another asking him what time it was. The man had no idea what awaited him, and was not looking when the drill bore a hole from one side of his knee to the other. It was not until the doctor lifted the smoking tool that the bewildered patient felt the pain, with a few second's delay. I remember the macabre dance and I am still trying to process it. However many times I go over it in my mind, in slow motion, step after step, the terrible *pax de deux* is impossible to assimilate.

I spent my days in bed, my perforated companion—a widower from the Ciociaria region south of Rome—in the bed next to me. This was my condition until, one evening, the ward on guard duty asked me if I wanted to go to the movies. I had no idea whether he was just being friendly or provoking me. After a while the whole contraption of my bed, with me in it, was wheeled into an outsized elevator and hauled up to the top floor of the hospital.

An enormous theater was filled with patients, in wheelchairs, or lying on their clinking beds tinkling with weights and counter-weights. They were all staring at a distant screen, waiting for the show to begin. The scene reminded me of those mesmerists in séance…That day, on the top floor of the Orthopedic Trauma Cinema, projected onto a sheet strung up haphazardly at the end of the hall, I saw the face of Louis De Funès[51] as ghostly and emaciated as an El Greco shroud. My leg stopped hurting, and all the other injured spectators were rapt, subjugated by the dark.

I sit at the movies, convalescing,
given
to a quiet physiotherapy,
to the exposure of a reflected glow.
The exchange is fervid,
I seek to be healed,
become the screen's screen, yield
the same vast presence of my body
to a lunar art. An absent bystander,
I am the patient of my passion
fixed in shared darkness
I observe the light's descent,
its catabasis.
I stop in a wood,
watch the film of snow
fall on the countryside, upon the crèche of
this artificial night, curving
over the mute theater
in the current of the story.
Eyeing that lit window,
I see someone pass behind the pane
signal my way,
signaling to all
the sick and invalid here, posing
for the group photo.[52]

XXXIX

In the end they decided to lower me into water. I was detached from my personal cable car and taken down to the ground floor where I was trussed up in a harness ready to be hooked onto a crane, which circled above my head before swooping down to lift me out of my wheel chair. Below me I could see people clutching at the edge of the pool. They couldn't swim. Their legs moved in slow motion, like jellyfish; clinging to the border they executed slow physiotherapy exercises—stylized bit-players in a minor landscape artist's painting. They commented on the human cargo as it transited over their heads. I was swinging in the air and the nurses were chatting to one another, a running commentary on the stages of the drop.

My feet were in the water, then my knees. I hadn't touched water for weeks. And I had never been officially launched. The miracle was that as soon as I touched the water I started to swim, as light, fast and free as a hydrometer on the surface of the water. Ah, sweet surface, cool surface! I was rid of my pins, lead discs and steel wires. No more locks and chains, no more weights. I was floating, I was dry, I was flying away. It didn't last long. They put an end to my flight before I crashed into the other patients, in that crazed pool game, which used rotulas and aching ivory as billiard balls.

XL

What about James Ensor's paintings then?[53] He was frenetically neurotic, an artist tortured by mystic visions and scatological obsessions, with a mania for stripping down flesh to the bone. Titles of his works include: *Skeleton Looking at Chinoiseries* (an impeccable skeleton-artist in his studio); *Skeleton Musicians* (a gathering of funereal orchestra players); *Skeletons Doing Children's Drawings* (where the innocent sketches are cast in a morbid light); against an acrid ochre background stick figure scrawls, *Skeletons Playing Billiards* (an excuse for contortions that mock classical statuary).

The paintings represent hyper-nudes, bodies stripped down to nothing, an X-ray vision. Ensor used skeletons as his braid of garlic to hold up against the Dracula of the Bourgeoisie. Like bunches of aromatic plants, his piles of bones were held to the nose of the general public and his critics in order to exorcise their evil, or at least hold it at bay. All you need to do is look at the painting, *Christ's Entry into Brussels,* to see the forms these evil powers took. Or study the drawings, *Haunted Furniture* or *Peculiar Insects*, or again *The Comical Smokers*, a portrait of two skulls, one smoking a pipe, the other a cigar.

The same surrealistic streak is evident in the painting *Dangerous Cooks*—Ensor depicts himself as a beheaded John the Baptist, his own artist's head on a platter beside a fish garnished with lemon. In the background the artist's enemies chat away while they dig in to their food.

A couple of canvases painted in 1890 or thereabouts top them all: *Self-Portrait as a Skeleton* and *My Portrait in 1960.* Both represent Ensor as he saw himself in the future. Projection and putrefaction work together so that the body 70 years in the future returns to its essential state, in fantastic skeleton livery. A direct descendent of Yorik, Ensor is the Huck' Finn of desolation.[54] He would be great dangling from a rear-view mirror, like a scoobie.

Note

Scoobies always come to mind when I think about my childhood:

Une dentelle s'abolit
Dans le doubte du Jeu supre^me[55]

Crocheting nothing from nothing is Mallarmé's equivalent of a scoobidou knot: braided plastic, a stylized, stretched-out little skeleton. As nonsensical and complex, enigmatic and vain as lace—especially the most extreme form of lace, which is poetry. Not bad for a kid's game from the 7/11 store. And what is the purpose of scoobies anyway? For dangling in the wind? For contemplating? For unbraiding?

Later, though, the vociferous prose writer answered the poet of silence regarding the meaning of lace: "their essential design, dots surrounded by holes... I know lace well, my mother used to sell it." [56]

XLI

Skulls were at home at my house. When I abandoned medical school my study materials must never have gotten tidied up. There were text books lying around, and yellowing paper that crumbled as soon as you touched it, but also various anatomical parts including, of course, skulls and cranial cavities. There were no plastic models in those days. Plastic is so reassuring in its representation of pure form with no content. Back then form and content were inseparable; bony hand in bony hand. It is hard to claim, for example, that the forehead is the "message" /"signifier" of its form. If you pick up and hold the brittle, spongy architecture of the occipital arc (a cross between a chocolate rice krispie cake and Roman *opus incertum*[57] you soon realize that its form coincides precisely with its content: "Form is simply content brought to the surface." [58] A skull is a lesson in esthetics, as well as a reminder always to consider the inside and the outside, and the before and after of the flesh on our body. Or, to put it differently, to consider the inside-first and outside-later that is the essence of the idea of the beyond. The words "interior"/"innards" comes to mind. When we listen to a shell we hear the echo of the sea. And when we listen to a skull? What resounds in the cranium? A river?

These morbid observations made me feel I would soon be receiving an eviction order. The person who occupies the apartment must decamp, disappear, strip the empty rooms of furnishings. A For Rent sign is already hanging outside. Projecting this thought into the future, we must all take into consideration—we really have no choice—that we might well end up as ornaments: we have bright futures as paper weights.

XLII

The years after the accident were the years I underwent sound traction. I probably chose to play the piano because it was already in the house. It was an orthopedic sound-box with a deformed keyboard and a tone worthy of a widow in the 1920s. This was the instrument I had at my disposal. It was like sticking your finger into an electric circuit: every note had a different voltage. For twelve years I plugged myself into the system, day after day, arpeggio after arpeggio. The source of electricity was the piano, and I became the instrument. Every afternoon, like the diligent student I was, I hooked up onto the grid. I plugged my finger-jacks into the right sockets and connected myself to the musical sound waves.

Reduced to being purely a medium, an electrical lead, I experienced my long daily sessions with the same spirit of resigned fervor that unites prayer and physiotherapy. What I was trying to cure myself of I am still not sure. And anyway, I was never cured. And yet, that unforgettable sensation of acoustic locomotion still lingers with me: the total passivity of the performer being pulled along by the music as he clings onto the keyboard for life. Like a water skier.

The sensation, I confess, was more dramatic when I played on a brand new baby grand, flashy as a Riva Aquarama off-shore speedboat, varnished mahogany and chrome dashboard, a wraparound windshield, 200 HP engines. Keys, levers and hammers, trills and leaps, the bass notes doubling up in the depths, vibrating pairs preparing to strike.

As for all the rest … the agony of the haltering practice sessions, the hobbling pieces… I dragged myself on for hours to no avail. I was incredibly jealous of a friend. He could spurt out perfect scales effortlessly, pearly notes strung together seamlessly on a silver string. I was never able to produce that kind of flow—one that gathers natural momentum but stays controlled. I expiated music.

XLIII

Yesterday, while I was moving house, I opened up a box and found all the X-rays I had had done when I was a child. Why had I put them away without even looking at them? This was a missed opportunity if ever there was one! It had taken forty years to gather together this collection of images, flora and fauna of my life, sitting there like trembling lemurs, or a bewildered assembly of ghosts.

Petals, or a condominium meeting. I pick the petals off an X-ray daisy. "I love myself…I love myself not". In fact there is only one ghost here, rustling through the plates:

"La vie vole de corps en corps, traqueé par leur faible dureé, come un oiseau traqué, qui fuit de branche en branche leur tremblente fragilité."[59]

Every page of that buried volume was a milestone marking the stages of my retreat, or rather my debacle. That is, the body's disintegration from the shy bird's-eye view of the creature in flight. I had all this material and I was about to throw it away! I possessed my own Pompeii! I had the negatives of my childhood! It was important at least to take a quick look at those original, delicate Calders[60]. Luminous calques of my body past. Body snatchers, ectoplasm and protoplasm I had attempted to ignore. (I remember once, while I was mountain walking, I found a fossil. I picked it up, looked at it for a second and was so tired that I threw it back down without thinking. I still regret it).

Am I being macabre here? These X-rays aren't really fossils. They are footprints of an organism that is still mutating and is therefore by no means extinct. They are a dead form of a form that is very much alive. An echo? More like feces. Childhood is like excrement, a give-away trail. Nothing like the vapor trails in the wake of an airplane. Just imagine! I could have stuck each and every one of these images in an album and flicked through them like a cartoon! I could have made a souvenir from the Body Cell Catacombs. I could have created my own Homeland Security. And I could have followed the growth of the shell—plasma membranes and teguments—the

Hermit Crab's cave growing with its prisoner inside it. I could have given sweet caresses to myself as my own son.

Primordial precursors of ancient civilizations were often killed because they were considered to be a kind of prototype. They were simply experimental versions of their progeny. Testing the ground. Testing … testing … testing…

Attachment

I can't seem to help it. Now I remember an afternoon spent clearing out shelves of books, records, cassettes. I stopped and listened to some tracks recorded years before, and suddenly the recording was interrupted half way through a song. Music gave way to silence, but a different silence to that produced by a virgin tape. In the absence of music there was the resounding emptiness of a household, mute but alive, and then, a clearing of the throat, distant noises, the shifting of a chair. I must have forgotten to turn the tape-recorder off. At one point a high pitched sound cut through the low rumble of background noises. From a faraway room you could hear the cry of a newborn baby.

You could hear it, or rather, the sound traveled across the house and was captured by the magnetic band that, in its turn, seized its tremulous sound. Like flypaper. Except that the little creature never dies. Au contraire, there is salvation from the passing of time. The little animal voice found a safe haven, survived the swim to the other bank rather than being swept away by the swollen river. Sticky-voice-saving-paper. Of course photographs serve the same function. But there's nothing that can compare with an audio reliquary. I am sitting here now and I can hear my son's voice at the age of two. I can't seem to help it. I'm scared of these archeological finds. So I can't wait to throw them away, and I'm already regretting it as I do so. Maybe because the regret is what gives me the strength to free myself of them once and for all.

These words of hers are little birds
of silence, the syllables ride on the water
of the spirit, trilling in bright waves
on the riptide[61]

XLIV

Going back to my long stay in hospital... though venial, there were quite a few consequences, not least of which an atrophied flexor muscle in the left foot. It was simply no longer there. A part of me, a part of my profile, however small, had vanished. Agnosia[62], alien parts of the body, all that. My perception of my big toe was that it had gone. The opposite of a phantom limb. In my case I was unable to see a part of my body to which I was still tied. It was there but it no longer belonged to me.

An unjustified absence of a segment of my own body. Alive and kicking, but invisible. I didn't get the sensation back until years later. Where had my big toe been all that time? In what kind of beyond-space had the alias of my big toe been wandering? Who is my big toe? To what extent does it belong to me? Or should I think of it as a lifeboat for this great ship of a body as it sails through life?

XLV

The reason I decided to dwell on the state of my big toe is because I wanted to use it as an introduction to the more worrying story of its side-kick—that is, its toe nail. I must admit, however, before going further, that I was partly responsible. Years before, in fact, I had accepted to translate some of d'Aurigny's poems. One of these recited:

O ongle plain de grand vertu
Ongle qui n'es jamais vestu
Sinon d'un gand souple et mignon
O ongle non pas ongle, non,
Mais fin chrital, qui vray amant
Estime plus que diamant.[63]

A finger nail full of virtue/A finger nail dressed in/a tiny delicate glove/a finger nail, no, not a finger nail/but a sliver of crystal the true lover/values more highly than a diamond

Shiny transparent finger nails, the poet added, were mirrors in which to gaze and admire oneself. Well-shaped nails, delightful nails, nails as masterpieces of nature. With its obsequious and predictable verses, *L'Ongle* would have been a perfect title for my story, but of course things were very different in my case. My toenail was far from being a source of pleasure, a fount of glory, or an onyx of grace for lovers. What happened is that my toenail underwent a slow and irreversible transformation. A deformed werewolf claw detached itself from the toe but did not drop off. Slowly drained of color, the streaked, twisted nail turned in on itself. As a bizarre Dantesque *contrapasso,*[64] rather than the delicate crystal described by d'Aurigny. I boasted a marbled keratin torch, dark lapis lazuli fashioned by some unknown Cosmatesque[65] old master craftsman.

(Previous incidents I feel it necessary to mention at this point include not so much the innumerable fingers caught in the doors of innumerable cars but more importantly the summer evening when, running into the sea, I stubbed my big toe on a rock and the nail split in two. I couldn't sleep at all that night; I tried to read but it was no good. All my energy and all my thoughts were sucked into that single, fluorescent plug-hole of pain. My blood, my attention, my curses—

everything coursed around that black pulsating object. I was at the center of my universe, but at my center was my big toe, and at the center of my big toe was a pure whirlpool of anti-matter which released indecipherable signals all night in the alphabet of a dead language).

I don't remember suffering particularly—the transformation took place without my really noticing—but one way or another I had to put an end to the mutation of my toenail. Hours, days, whole weeks out of a decade given over to diagnoses.

The medical explanations I received were not very convincing. One school of thought found the cause to be mechanical, and consequently ordered X-rays, stress tests, and examinations of past traumas and present posture. Another school, the majority, focused on fungal or bacterial infections and called for a wide range of tests, blood and urine samples, the application of creams and unguents for months and months, using droppers, brushes, and sand paper. It was DIY for my own body, but to no avail. One doctor came up with a new idea: after applying the night cream I was to wrap the toe up in cling wrap. I did precisely that, and prayed I would not die in my sleep. I was convinced that, if the unfortunate circumstance of my death were to take place, the plastic wrapping would be seen as part of some obscure satanic rite (a dead man with his left big toe allusively bandaged, perhaps facing East, a disciple of the clawed Anubis).

Later on I tried out a Humanist doctor, who knew a great deal of jargon and dabbled in the esoteric. He impressed me with clever word games, but my toe nail was still a wreck. A further attempt was with a bald doctor, a true bibliophile, whose approach was straightforward. He pulled a volume of an encyclopedia entitled *Nails* from his shelf, sat down next to me, and started to leaf through it. In a kind of police lineup, he invited me to pick out the culprit among hundreds of suspects. Page after page, images of the most disaster-stricken nails in the planet paraded in front of me—an interminable gallery of keratin sculptures in every possible shape and form. Gemstones, in their way, a multicolored lapidary. I suffered from 'idiopathic dystrophy', it was concluded, or rather—the final word—'unexplained onycholysis'. In my notes I find the expression 'half and half nails.' This can't be a technical term, can it? Even if it isn't, I'll leave it.

XLVI

Tours of the tombs of Pierre and Marie Curie[66] have been suspended. The visits used to take place in small groups under the supervision of a guide with a Geiger counter. When the group gathered, the guide would ask them to step aside so that he could calculate the level of radiation in the crypt. The bones let off plenty of it, it seems. After years, the skeletons of the couple were still crackling with radioactivity, rays flashing as if from a buried solar monstrance. From that life source, a continuous, sinuous wave. Radiological angels, together in the dark.

XLVII

Talking of darkness, when I was very young, I used to live in an apartment with rooms that wrapped around a courtyard. We were on the fifth floor, and the parapets on the windows were far too low. I still have the feeling I lived for years in the presence of a magnet. The whole house leant sideways. The depth of this domestic abyss was only about sixty feet but it felt like much more—especially when it was time to hang the washing out. The washing line looked like ship's bunting. Or worse—a blueprint for an impossible, yet imminent, challenge. For hours and hours our young Perceval would stare at the line knowing the Grail was on the other side. The emptiness called out from below, compelling, excruciating, irresistible. I tried to imagine myself diving right into the hanging tablecloth. I simulated the terror of it. I practiced my fear assiduously.

(A real dive, from a thirty-foot springboard: the future perfect tense of the pool's surface, curving into the subjunctive mood of doubt, the conditional mood of anguish, the imperative of exhortation, only to end in the sovereign infinitive, the verb to fly. The attraction I felt—when I stared at the drop during the endlessly eventless afternoons of my childhood—stemmed from the possibility of stretching out that instant in time, cracking it like a walnut, extracting the kernel of inebriating giddiness, swanning yet swooning. I understand the taste for canyoning and base jumping, free climbing and rafting. I envy bungee jumpers and watch sky surfers with unlimited admiration, tinged with panic. It's a matter of how you conjugate your verbs. Extreme sports and drugs are just grammatical shifts. A debilitating escape into the kingdom of an infinite present tense.)

(A real sky-dive. Now you're talking. A dishcloth suspended mid-air, nothing to hold it but two pegs. A plant ripped out of the ground, uprooted. I've never spent so long observing my feet).

XLVIII

I'm having a problem getting a booking to go inside the CNN studios in Atlanta, so I decide to go to the Cyclorama instead. Half-way between a *son et lumière* show and a planetarium, between a Rotor ride and a merry-go-round, the installation is a 42 feet tall barrel with a 358 feet circumference, painted between 1885 and 1886. The giant work of art represents the Battle of Atlanta, when Union forces razed the capital of Georgia. Spectators sit in the dark in a mobile amphitheater placed like a cone at the center of the cylinder. A precursor of cinema, the show goes through the same motions but the other way round: it is not the film that moves but the audience. The images on the screen are completely still and we become the movie by being set in motion.

The room starts circling anti-clockwise, while recorded music and running commentary animate the scenes. A complex array of theatre lights illuminate the areas of the canvas we are supposed to focus our attention on as we pass by—to no avail. The whole circuit takes thirty minutes, but the mechanism feels so dated that after barely three minutes people start to get bored. For us creatures of the twentieth century, there can be no such thing as an unbroken storyline. We require variations, pauses, tacking, threads tying together, back-stitching. The uninterrupted drawn strip of the Cyclorama is as unfathomable to us today as the continuous frieze spiraling up Trajan's Column.

The long, rotating sequence slowly draws to a close. The guide points out significant features of the painting, the odd curiosity: the only woman, a dying Clark Gable look-alike, a few images in bass-relief, a group of painted chalk figures, a little mouse. Trumpets, drums, shouts. A kid asks his parents how much longer to go. Then, suddenly, dead silence. Pitch black.

The nineteenth-century fairground display has ground to a halt, broken. The unplanned event creates suspense and we all hold our breath. In this artificial and unexpected night, our theater seats go on spinning, as unstoppable as a satellite lost in space or a roulette wheel without a ball.

A few words are exchanged in low whispers as we wait. The dervish is still swirling. If, as I claimed, the Cyclorama has transformed us into a movie, then the film on the reel must have split. Now I can truly say that I don't regret missing the CNN studios. I came to Atlanta to witness the glorious future of television, and here I am—to my great surprise—wandering with no direction through the anguished infancy of cinema. Or should I say its gestation?

XLIX

Another cyclorama. The circle of mountains in the backdrop are the landscape I hold dearest: my mandibular arch, and the peaks are my teeth. But there is a problem. The glaciers are receding, and the amphitheatres of moraine are higher and drier than ever before. The whole range is contracting like a retractable claw. That was when I started a three year campaign of dentistry. Polishing, pulling and plugging were no longer options because my gums were leaving me. You could call the grimace a periodontic snigger, with the curtain always open. As if inhabited by an alien smile, constantly aimed at an imaginary friend (who must have been very amusing to have caused such a constant sneer), my teeth were always on show in their full, panoramic and dazzling glory. Fire signals along the coast.

The real song and dance, however, took place at night when I had nothing better to do than clench my jaws in exhausting spasms of teeth gnashing. My bed was a workshop, clanging and creaking as enamel struck whetstone. Sparks flew. My teeth would grind in a hypnotically regular rhythm, like maracas. What unconscious beat was I responding to? Who was playing me?

The first attempt to cure my habit, known as sleep bruxism, consisted in a mouth guard, an elaborate plastic and steel shell that fits into your palate. But the remedy was unsuccessful and I was forced to undergo surgery. The name of the procedure was fancy, something like radotage, tricotage or curettage—I don't remember. What I soon found out was that the name was simply a way to mask the brutality of the secateurs. Because that's what this operation was about: pruning back the purple vine of my gums.

Edward Scissor Hands works between the teeth. Snip, snip, he splices and knits the blood-soaked threads into a string of lace. Now the white cliffs of Dover rise high, shining brightly in the sun, the chalk walls newly enameled. There they are, far away, seeing travelers off on their journeys. So long! Farewell!

L

So much for my teeth. In the meantime, however, in the hemisphere of my knees there was an ongoing process of erosion of the rotula, a quiet tinkling of crystal glasses. It's snowing inside me. Flakes flutter and fall, slowly floating as if there were no wind. Let me try and rewind the whole of my past and envisage it from below, from a subjective view point, the lens half way down my leg. Because that is the place, that is the position designated to shape my life. To start with just knocks, bangs, and breaks; later, gradual pulverization, accompanied by popping and cracking, autumnal crunching and crackling, "sanglots longs[67]"—what in medical jargon is known as 'crepitus'. (This may be why I am still fascinated by the way kids sit on the floor, as if their joints were basculating, and as if they would enjoy an infinite life with them. It looks as though their destiny is infinite, or at least proportionate to the extension of their meniscus.)

. . . blind and still
the knee rests in the leg.[68]

Well, rest is not exactly the right word. My knee totters and topples, the rusty pulley creaks as it sinks into the deep well of my flesh. The corrosion has been so gradual it is imperceptible. In fact, I was quite surprised when the electric switch finally blew that day my knee was no longer able to absorb the shock. Let me be precise here. The image I conjured up was not of the meniscus, but of one of those modern cupboards whose drawers glide silently in and out on perfectly designed runners consisting of a plastic track inlaid with hundreds of little pulleys. It was one of these that snapped that day. My knee swung uselessly, and the whole modular cupboard fell to pieces.

Back to the operating theater, but this time it was hi-tech. Not for me the shadowy narcosis of a total anesthetic. I received a quick, friendly rush of pain killer right into the area where it was needed. Euphoria, lightness, visibility. Archaic practices had been set aside once and for all, together with chalk spare parts, iron plates, steel corsets and traction pulleys.

The doctors asked if I wanted to watch the operation on the screen—the film, they said, would be about twenty minutes—and I accepted gladly. Tied to the mast, wax blocking my ears, I would finally get the chance to see the screeching sirens from within, the shrieking voices of my cartilage, the shrill night visitors, the chattering sisters. So there I was on a bed, eyes on a monitor, a background noise of pincers and pumps. And suddenly there was light. The dark amphitheater of my knee was struck by a ray of light from the mini camera that been inserted into my body. A floodlight in the mine shaft.

I had entered, and could finally examine closely the rich lode under the knee-cap, the side tunnels into which the blood was sucked back by a frenetic aspirator, the tenacious tool cutting and shaping the hair style of white algae. An aquarium, voices, the fish that is my eye swimming slowly against the warm tropical currents of my leg. A hypnotic underwater flow, mingled with nausea. Two hours' dive and the viewing turns into a nightmare, but now that I'm here I can't stop watching. This is the first time I've had the chance to be Narcissus bending over his reflection in the water and admiring his own features.

The circular stare of the serpent that eats its own tail has been set on me. The Egyptian and Neo-Platonic *Ouroboros*[69] has returned in a parody of a patient scrutinizing a screen to see the inside-out glove of his own body. I exist, I am on track, but the track is a Möbius strip where inside and outside change places as you look at it. From its dark bruised depths, from its iridescent cavern, my Knee stares at me having called me in with the feeble excuse of arthroscopic surgery. The Blue Cave.

I can't bear its staring at me any longer. The voices are deafening, and the search for new passages under my skin intolerable. I feel like a space ship with mechanical failure which is stuck in orbit, four floating astronauts messing about with the damaged control panel. This video is evidence that I am mere plankton, that I have disappeared into thin air.

LI

The Biodôme is neither a zoo, nor an aquarium, park or botanical garden.[70] The dazzling white building—its name, like Savinio's book,[71] literally meaning 'the house of life'—resembles a vast glass and cement carapace, a turtle shell without the turtle. Or rather, in the place of a turtle there is a replica of the Garden of Eden, a living museum, Noah's Ark.

The model is the Earth itself. Emptied and cleaned out like the inside of a shell, the circular space of the Olympic velodrome is divided into four areas: a massive four seasons pizza[72], each quarter slice of which represents a different ecosystem. In the space of an hour you cross a Brazilian equatorial forest, a North American wilderness, a polar landscape, and the underwater habitat of the St. Lawrence River. The ticket collector's explorer headwear should have served as a warning, but I was unprepared for the breathtaking sight when the heavily insulated door opened in front of me. A blast of hot, humid air hits me. The rainforest is pulsating with transplanted and simulated life. Following a steamy path filled with puddles, I admire the luxurious vegetation. Some of the towering trees turn out to be fake, with air vents on their plastic trunks, but the rest is real enough. Waterfalls, beaches, a troop of monkeys, floating crocodiles. In a cave close by hundreds of bats behind glass beat their wings and shriek.

In the Laurentian forest the climate changes. Judging from the poplar leaves it must be Spring. Shivering, I walk around a lake teeming with fish, a screen meanwhile showing the inside of a beaver's den, filmed with hidden cameras the guide explains. Panopticon and animal candid camera: it's as if George Orwell's terrible prophesies were super-imposed, *Animal Farm* transposed to *1984*.

The height of the building is dizzying. There are over 150 feet of clear sky-seeming space filled with birds. Light rains in as if it were a greenhouse, but actually the main sources of light are dozens of spotlights and reflectors. Finally I understand what was producing the noise I originally thought came from the Amazonian fauna. The buzzing was made by Technology that hovers around the oversized body of Ecology, as a doctor would with a patient.

Patiently the forest cooks under the droning spotlights. The Biodôme feels like a microwave oven. Or rather, an incubator. The space for life is actually an oxygen tent where medical science in the most sophisticated manner it has at its disposal attempts to delay a body's decay. I see visions of explants and surgical operations. A face-lift for the planet? Artificial waves. Alienated penguins. Fake ice and wind. Now we're in a refrigerator. No, we're inside one of those souvenirs: a glass dome with snow inside. Shake it and the snowflakes fall.

LII

After yet another period of convalescence, I was advised not to move around too much, not to run, and not to play any violent sports so that my bones could heal properly without further trauma. I was up in the mountains that winter and I decided I wanted to go riding. Against a backdrop of tall, dark fir trees, the pounding of hooves was muffled by snow, no louder than drumming fingers on a tabletop. Rocking gently from side to side, the horse hardly needed reigning in. It's black haunches, as I dismounted, were steaming, shaking, foaming, towering darkly above me. And that's when the fun started.

After weeks of immobility, my muscles were no longer up to the challenge. As soon as I was on the ground I realized—to my horror—that my legs were stuck in the position they had adopted in the saddle. I stood there, bust forward, back ramrod straight and knees splayed around an imaginary quadruped. A plasticine model skeleton. I looked like a toy cavalry soldier who had lost its war horse. Unable to walk, I was taken home and home I stayed, sitting by the fire to thaw, a log among logs, contemplating my latest metamorphosis. This was me, still me, of course. Living Play-doh, with incredibly slow reactions. That evening, finally, one muscle sent out a signal. My calf started to shake, the spell was lifted, and my biological functions slowly returned to normal.

(One could claim, I suppose, that this solemn macro-cramp was the crowning moment of a long series of cramps. Obsessed by the legend that lactic acid is absorbed by the body, I would imagine my feet contracting, my toes deforming, under the effect of some kind of monstrous cheesy secretion. I would feel my blood turn to cream cheese, blocking my arteries, paralyzing my nerves one by one. I envisaged an assortment of dairy products filling my tissues, amalgamating my muscles, filtering the frightening serum of fatigue, the disheartening serum of truth. Luckily I've felt the vise-hold of lactic acid only once in my life, in my upper thigh. When it strikes there's nothing you can do to loosen its grip. There's no point in pushing or pulling, stretching or twisting. I was stuck there, thrashing about uselessly, racked by jarring pain as my hamstring was plucked like a violin string.)

LIII

And then the head came off. The decapitated head of my femur.

A beheaded leg. Three days after the operation, the altar-boy/surgeon held up a plastic ciborium which contained the consecrated host, my body.

I flinched. When I looked more closely, however, I realized the shock did not stem from those poor remains. I could look and look, examine carefully that detached part of me, my divided self, and I still wouldn't understand who was looking at whom (the body part in the cup was inanimate, with the docility of an animal).

What startled me, surprisingly, was a sharp stab of pain from the other side. A slab of steak, rare, blue. It reeked of steak. I reeked of steak. So that's what I always smell like, inside? My cellophane-thin layer of flaccid skin is the only thing that holds in the dreadful butcher's stench, the belly-full of blood you can smell from the cellar, as it wafts up from an underground network of veins.

LIV

Sleep

Now I know why I twist and turn so much in bed. Every year I feel like there's a new pattern, an ecliptic imperceptibly modifying the path of the sun. One more rotation before finally dropping off, the blankets gripping me in their vise hold. A stripped screw in a soft plank. Worse, a forkful of spaghetti gyrating on a plate all night, the strings hopelessly tight, then loose—my flesh. And my mind turns to the earth's orbit, the skewer of the earth slowly turning to roast itself in the sun.

*

At other times, when I am relaxed, I wait patiently for the shuttle bus that will take me to sleep after work. The bus stop is empty, the somnibus is late.

(Another variation. The removals truck has arrived. I start loading it, but I can't seem to fit all my fatigue inside it. I don't' have the energy to pack it all tightly into the available space. The workers complain and call me off the job, and the truck takes off without me. I am left standing on the sidewalk surrounded by boxes. Next time it'll go better.)

*

I lie awake. The tide of my breathing. High and low. Boredom. A colony of bi-valves grips onto the rock that is me. The waves wash over them, submerging them then slowly pulling away again. Mussels on the body-rock.

*

My sleep has become a bone the night dogs gnaw and leave to the morning dogs.

*

Phantoms and specters scamper all over. A haunted castle. Apparitions, incursions. I feel their passage. I suffer their presence. Slamming doors. How can an organism infested with thoughts ever sleep? How can one sleep in an organism infested with thoughts?

The ghosts remind me of those joke candles. The birthday boy blows on the candles, they go out and then come to life, again, and again, and again. The indomitable flame rears its head every time. I'm just the same. I can't blow myself out. When everything seems finally to have been tamed, in some part of my body there is always that spark that refuses to die out. Happy birthday to you, Happy birthday to you… and the cake is alight once again.

*

Sleep is like a twisted rag, wet with sleep. However hard you twist it, it is still heavy with water. A never-ending process: there'll always be another drop to mangle.

*

A nightmare: a planetary stock exchange. What would happen if sleeping at night were linked to the Dow Jones index? Sleep only when shares are up; when they drop, back to insomnia. The individual totally subsumed by the laws of the market. That's when I woke up.

*

I tune into sleep as if I were searching for a radio channel. Medium wave or short wave. But I can't seem to find the frequency.

*

Hangnails. Those little flaky bits of skin are like antennae. Messages sent out to extraterrestrial civilizations.

The craters created by mouth ulcers along the rift of my lower lip. The sores are like volcanic lakes—Bracciano, Bolsena, Nemi.

I break things. I tempt them to damage themselves. In my presence things cave in. I invite fracture and fissure. Look at this table, for instance.

LV

Infancy of a father

It all started with an April breeze. Blowing lightly on my face—I must have been seven or eight—I felt the first buds of a rash break out. It was the breath of measles, a foretaste of the blossoming of ailments that was to follow. From that day on my body bore fruit, a veritable orchard of seasonal disorders.

> (*Bottled fruit, vertebrae stuck together like prunes in the larder box, animal sugars, soft cartilage, syrupy peaches in their jar. I tenderize, season, transform myself. A long shiver, and billions of cells, wave after wave, replace one another, causing mutations in the material they are made out of. But everything is so gradual, so gentle, that the little meander they have slowly carved and then filled in is practically unchanged. I myself, then, am made up of the same words as many years ago, but with new letters, altered syllables. I am an army in the midst of battle, where reservists jump in to replace the slain. I am an old suit, patched with the same cloth, the stitching visible. I am a loom of flesh, "molecules shuttled to and fro."*[73])

That's enough now. Whooping cough is looming. My tree is being shaken, bending lower with every paroxysm. The cure is a period of rest at the top of the Gran Sasso mountain.

Towards the end of the 1960s this rustic *Zauberberg* was completely cut off from the world, desolate and dispirited. Poor and bare. We stayed in the same vast hotel where the brutal Otto Skorzeny successfully carried out Operation Oak in 1943, the rescue mission that freed the pathetic deposed puppet dictator, Mussolini. Thinking back to those freezing, empty, silent rooms, and that stony, echoing landscape, the emaciated face of the overthrown tyrant, his weak jaw set in false virility, is immediately conjured up. Like Goya's Pelele,[74] the effigy. Like a colored rag doll thrown in the air by a group of women, bouncing off a washing line, he went on smiling, without ever making eye contact. He greeted people blankly, nodded at nothing. No contact whatsoever.

I start my prescribed daily walks, and my coughing fits started to abate. I can picture myself, standing—the very image of a country boy—against a backdrop greener than usual. The Nazis are still there, I can hear them, which transports me into a scene from The Sound of Music. Nature is everywhere, but it is laced with anxiety and asthma. Slow-paced family excursions followed by long afternoons playing table soccer. The Italians call it *calcio balilla*, which harks back to Fascist Balilla youth organization—Mussolini again. I spend hours curved over the handles, some of the waiters winking at me, as if to give me permission. In an enormous games room, practically an air hangar, high ceilinged and almost entirely empty, I count out the afternoons of my rest cure, patiently awaiting the return to normality. The ball ricochets off the table, bounces along the deserted corridors that witnessed the German air-borne raid, and finally comes to a halt in the company of dust balls under some cupboard or other. Am I getting any better, I wonder?

Many years later I read some disturbing news: underneath that same mountain they were setting up a nuclear research laboratory. That makes three things. How can I join the dots between Mussolini, the passion for table soccer and the auscultation of quarks? Is there, per chance, a table soccer game of elementary particles deep under the mountain? Or, again, might those red and blue plastic soccer players, lined up along their steel rods, be competing to scalp the Dictator as if they were Aztec warriors?

Sacrificial rites, initiations, death and regeneration of cosmos. Or simply the Ruins of Kasch[75] in the town of Cascia—a homely *teatrum mundi* in the Appenines. Or again, a scene from *Apocalyse Now*: Kurt emerging from an expedition in the Abruzzi mountains like a Priest King destined to be sacrificed (wasn't it true that he traded in ivory? By extension, could the bald man be a representation of a table soccer ball?) Here's another image: a peasant Marlon Brando playing a part in the Golden Bough.[76] The head of the Mafia Boss.[77] But that's another story.

A Fascist sympathizer years later secretly showed me a talisman, holding it up against the light. He called it the 'capo del Capo'. It was a pommel, a simple brass knob the household used to tie back the sitting room curtains, the taboo profile hidden inside it. A silhouette of the Dictator's big head. (What amazing passementerie!

The furniture trimmings of a myth. It must have taken some skill—worthy of the secret services—to hide a totem of this kind in a curtain pommel. The Holy Face in a counter-weight. A perverse charade being acted out between the 'muslin' curtains and Mussolini. As in Poe's story, *The Purloined Letter*, the Italian family was hiding its secret in plain sight, making it even more evident. The curtain fastening mechanism meant it was handled often: all it needed was someone to say "open the curtains" and—hey presto!—there was a flag raising ceremony.) It was not until much later that I came face to face with a life-size, bronze bust of the man. A famous doctor was checking to make sure a broken bone had set, and there in the middle of his surgery was the effigy, looking down at me over the doctor's shoulder.

> *There is no doubt that at the time the original bust was cast the model could not have imagined that the Gran Sasso raid would one day take place. Considering what the future held for him, this boastful figure at the height of his power inspires pity. His destiny was to run away dressed as a clown-soldier. Or maybe it was all an artifice from the start—and there is the tragedy. Acting the part of someone you are not; not living up to your responsibilities. It was even rumored that he dressed up as a woman to escape capture. Really? It feels right somehow. To the bitter end. How could anyone have taken him seriously? There is still something familiar in his surly expression. It's no joke, I know, but he played with fire all the time, and ended up being his own caricature, Chaplin's Bonito Napoloni. I can now appreciate the horror of the brass knob. It depicts his face at Piazzale Loreto*[78]*, the terrible counter-weight of his body-curtain hanging from his feet. Strung up beef carcasses, bats on a branch, a mysterious plant drinking the light of day. (His lover was also hung out on the line. There's another product of history ripe for the picking.) Marguerite Yourcenar once commented, in fact, that Mussolini died in the twentieth century the death of a third century emperor.*[79]
>
> *His face again: carved into the rocks high up at the Furlo mountain pass, one hundred meters of his profile. A petit-bourgeois form of earth divination, topographically placed so that his lover could see him from her little room in the valley where he used to stop*

off on his trips between Rome and Riccione. The modest hotel with its restaurant and printed postcards—"Benito Mussolini slept in this bedroom", or "Il Duce ate in this dining room"—is a shrine. The Furlo Pass is Italy's Mount Rushmore, with all the same consequences.

His big head yet again: like an Easter Island statue, or the Black Stone of the Kaaba, the Gran Sasso mountain of a panicked populace. He was the opposite of Samson. His strength lay in his naked pate, his power and presumption apparent in its sheer size. It was four-dimensional: height x width x length x strength. It was also magnetic, reassuringly like an ox skull, to the extent that families felt protected, while behind the scenes folically-endowed side-kicks brandished their batons, wild beasts and torturers in their trucks. (In Cascia there's a piazza Magrelli, the square dedicated to an uncle who was tortured. Uncles and ungues, nails torn out of their fingers. As a child I could almost hear their cries, and suffered terribly.) But he denied any knowledge of what went on. Nobody ever told him. If they had, he would no doubt have sorted things out. His bonhomie gave people a glimmer of hope, and that was his most ignominious trait. The doubt that assailed the crowds was that, in the end, all things given, he would have been on your side.

Stockholm Syndrome. He was like a father, and Italy had for the first time sent its King into exile (no such thing as a sword, of course! He was reduced to being a garden gnome, little dwarf Sleepy taking a rest on the garden path.) The British sentenced Charles I to death, Louis XVI was sent to the guillotine, and then, at the end of a long line, there are the Italians. We are cowards; we lack the courage to take the capitis diminutio[80] *to its extreme conclusion. Mussolini's execution was clandestine, fearful and prudish. Devious and hot-headed, singularly unable to hit the nail on the head, we ended up with a head on the ground. But we didn't touch it or get our hands dirty. No, we used our shoes. Leaving aside Umberto Saba's claim that Italians are fratricides not parricides,*[81] *after Romulus and Remus, after the* Contra tyrannos[82]*, and after signing the Treaty of Rome, we can finally say we are Europeans. The single market for Assassinated Fathers.*

Let's return to the bronze statue. To cut a long story short, while the bust of Mussolini is staring down at me, the doctor decides he needs further information and prescribes an MRI. A month later, as I wait my turn, the radiologist to whom I had previously delivered my bio-data bursts into the room, out of breath. Had I perchance omitted to tell him I had cadmium-titanium screws inside my body? Don't I realize what could happen to my body during an electromagnetic test? There are stories of forgotten watches smashing into a thousand pieces and strewn in a radius of up to ten yards from the machine. Of torn arms, of lacerated wrists. Of a workman carrying a pail of iron filings—the ones drawn on a magnet—who accidentally entered the radiology room and was blown away. What else? Well, the story of me ending up in that cubicle, lying in the dark like an Egyptian mummy on the banks of the river of time, the screws unscrewing themselves from my bones, pulled out by a magnetic force, and becoming little space ships orbiting in the hyperspace, a magic blender of shards.

I never saw the medical luminary again, nor his bronze bust. I never went back to the Gran Sasso. And yet I still ponder over why Mussolini's execution feels like that of a Christian martyr. Upside down. St. Peter.[83] Too secret and yet over exhibited. Or under exhibited and not very secret. Neither an ambush nor the stocks. Neither authoritative nor compassionate. Or, more simply, upside down, like the dangling corpse. Timidly proclaimed, ruthlessly inclement. I'm not interested in history, but in my ailments, their crystallization, calculus, the renal sand of our dreams. My infancy was spent in the company of a shadow. I was born after a regicide.

Notes

1. Plato, *Phaedrus* IV, 229-230

2. Literally a 'guide of souls', in Jungian philosophy the psychopomp was a mediator between the conscious and the unconscious.

3. *Hegel's Science of Logic*, George Allen & Unwin, 1969, Translated by A.V.Miller

4. Sigmund Freud, *The Interpretation of Dreams*, Macmillan, N.Y. 1913. Freud concluded that he was subconsciously trying to absolve himself of his own sense of guilt for not curing Irma completely. In his dream, Irma says: "If you only knew what pains I've got now in my throat and stomach and abdomen—it's choking me."

5. W.H. Auden , *Goodbye to the Mezzo Giorno*, Encounter, Nov. 1958

6. Kant, *The Critique of Judgement*, Oxford, 1952 Translated by James Creed Meredith

7. The Ancient Greek philosopher, Artemidorus, wrote his *Interpretation of Dreams* in the second century AD. The text later became a reference point for Michel Foucault's *History of Sexuality*, vol. 3. 'The Care of the Self'. Gallimard 1990

8. Nessus was the third centaur. In Greek mythology, Deianeira poured Nessus's 'magic' blood onto Herakles's under-garments as revenge for his infidelity. The effect was intense burning, then the cloth sticking to the skin, then deification.

9. In Italian the expression *mano morta* means when someone uses their hands inappropriately, for example feeling someone up on a crowded bus.

10. Samuel Butler, *Erewhon*, Chapter XXIV. London, Jonathan Cape, 1921

11. The battle took place in 778 in a mountain pass between France and Spain where Charlemagne's forces suffered defeat by the Basques. The battle was narrated in both *The Song of Roland* and *Orlando Furioso*

12. Magrelli, unpublished. My translation.

13. T.S. Eliot, *The Waste Land* , Part IV (1922). New York, Horace Liveright

14. Magrelli, *Contagion of Matter*, translated by Anthony Molino.

Holmes and Meier, NY, 2000. p.8-9

15. In geology, amygdales (or amygdules) are formed by secondary minerals filling cavities in igneous rocks such as basalt.

16. Théophile Gautier (1811-1872) in *The Escurial*, translated by C.F.Bates

17. A vessel for exhibiting an object of piety.

18. Latin for 'principle of individuation'. "'Just as in a stormy sea, unbounded in every direction, rising and falling with howling mountainous waves, a sailor sits in a boat and trusts in his frail barque: so in the midst of a world of sorrows the individual sits quietly supported by and trusting in his *principium individuationis*. Friedrich Nietzsche, 'The Birth of Tragedy', Russell & Russell 1964

19. Virginia Woolf, *Mrs. Dalloway*, London, Hogarth Press, 1925

20. *aufsatz* means a composition or essay, while *aussatz* means leprosy.

21. French poet (1762-1794), guillotined for 'crimes against the state' during the French Revolution.

22. Avenues, paths, crossroads and administrative districts.

23. Over a hundred acres.

24. Yves Montand (1921-1991), Italian-born naturalized French actor and singer.

25. In the Italian Magrelli uses the phrase *L'Ape di Ade*. An *Ape* is an Italian three-wheeled utility vehicle, and also a bee. *Ade* is Hades.

26. Literally 'City of Light' , but the phrase also refers to Paris, center of Enlightenment ideas.

27. Kleist, Über *das Marionettentheater.* 1810. The essay was first published in four installments in the daily BerlinerAbendblatter from December 12 to 15, 1810. Kleist was editor of the newspaper.

28. Sydenham's Chorea is a medical condition, historically called Dance of Saint Vitus, characterized by jerky, hyperkinetic movements.

29. Magrelli, *The Contagion of Matter*. Porta Westfalica p.47. *Op. cit.*

30. Joseph Joubert, *Les Carnets*, ed. Andreé Bauenier. Paris, Gallimard,1938.

31. Ludwig Feuerbach (1804-1872), *Thoughts on Death and Immortality*. (1980). Translated from the German by James A. Massey. Univer-

sity of California Press. Berkeley and Los Angeles

32. Edmund Spenser, A.C. Hamilton, ed., Edmund Spenser, *The Faerie Queene* (London: Longman, 1977), p. 253 n. (on 2.8.32.6-9): "Port Esquiline [was] a gate in ancient Rome, its anus as it gave passage to the common dump."

33. In Hegel's philosophy, the German term refers to when a thesis and an antithesis interact, and is often translated as 'sublate'

34. Gabriele D'Annunzio, ''Il secondo amante di Lucrezia Buti,' in *Le faville del maglio*, Volume 1 Milan, Fratelli Treves Editori , 1924

35. René Leriche, French surgeon and pain specialist. Quoted in C.Canguilhem, On the Normal and the Pathological p.46 D.Reidel, Dordrecht, Holland (1978).

36. Danish astronomer (1546-1601)

37. An area in Sardinia full of caves which became notorious during the wave of kidnappings in the 1960s and 1970s.

38. *Colpo della strega* is a sudden and intense back pain. The word for 'witch' (strega) is also the name of a company that produces a popular liqueur and chocolates.

39. André Breton in *Le surréalisme e la peinture* Paris, N.R.F., 1928

40. Magrelli, *The Contagion*, p.112, *Op. cit.*

41. Alberto Giacometti (1901-1966) , Surrealist sculptor and painter.

42. Yves Bonnefoy , *Alberto Giacometti: A Biography of His Work*, Paris, Flammarion, 2006

43. In Italian the expression 'giacomo giacomo' means shaky. This is a play on Giacometti's name.

44. Ibid.

45. Ibid.

46. Ibid.

47. In bull-fighting, the swing of the cape. Named after St. Veronica, who, according to Christian legend, wiped Christ's brow with a cloth as he passed by on his way to Golgotha.

48. Giorgio de Santillana and Herthan von Dechend, *Hamlet's Mill*, Gambit, 1969. The book deals with history, mythology and archeoastronomy.

49. Valerio Magrelli, *The Contagion*. p.. 103, *Op. cit.*

50. Francisco Ferreras, known as Pipín , born in Cuba in 1962, holds world records for 'no limits' free-diving.

51. Louis de Funès (1914-1983), French film actor of Spanish origin.

52. Valerio Magrelli, *Instructions on How to Read a Newspaper and Other Poems*. Ed. Anthony Molino. Translated by Riccardo Duranti, Annamaria Crowe Serrano, Anthony Molino. New York, Chelsea Editions, , 2009

53. James Ensor (1860-1949), Belgian expressionist and surrealist painter and print-maker.

54. In the Italian text Magrelli uses the name Gian Burrasca. *Il diario di Gian Burrasca*, by Vamba, the pen-name of Luigi Bertelli, was published in installments in a Sunday paper in 1907-8. The protagonist's nickname, Gian Burrasca, "Hurricane Johnny", has become a proverbial way to describe a restless, 'terrible' boy.

55. Stéphane Mallarmé, *Poésies*. Editions de la revue indépendente, Paris 1887. The lines are translated into English by John Knowles as "The supreme play of doubt denies a lace that opens."

56. Robert Poulet, *Entretiens familiers avec L. F. Céline*. Paris, Plon 1958. The vociferous prose writer is Céline.

57. An ancient Roman construction technique where irregular shaped stones were placed on a bed of Roman cement.

58. La forme c'est le fond qui rimonte à la surface".Victor Hugo, *Proses philosophiques de 1860-65*, in Victor Hugo (1802-1885) in Œuvres *complètes. Critique*, Robert Laffont, éd. Jean-Pierre Reynaud, coll. Bouquins, Paris.

59. Paul Valéry, *Mauvaises Penseés e autres*, Cahiers du Sud. José Corti, Paris 1941. Life flies from body to body, hunted by their feeble duration, as a hunted bird flees from branch to branch their trembling fragility. My translation.

60. American sculptor and painter (1898-1976). Calder is best known for his mobiles and stationary sculptures he called stabiles, as well as for his miniature moving wire toys

61. Valerio Magrelli, *Poesie e altre poesie*. Children's Corner. Turin, Einaudi, 1996. (My translation).

62. A psycho-neurological condition that impedes your ability to recognize objects or people, smells or sounds, while none of your senses are defective.

63. D'Aurigny. *Poètes du XVI siècle*. Paris, Pléaide, 1953. "A finger nail full of virtue/A finger nail dressed in/a tiny delicate glove/a finger nail, no, not a finger nail/but a sliver of crystal the true lover/values more highly than a diamond." (My translation).

64. Dante Alighieri, *The Inferno*. Literally, 'Opposite suffering.'

65. A style of inlayed stonework typical of Medieval Italy, and especially in Rome.

66. Pierre and Marie Curie were moved from Sceaux to the Panthéon in Paris and buried together in 1995. For fear of radiation the coffins were clothed in lead.

67. Paul Verlaine (1844-1896). *Poèmes saturniens*. 1866. Paris, Pléiade. "Les sanglots longs/Des violons/De l'automne" The long sobs of the violins of Autumn.

68. Valerio Magrelli, *Ora serrata retinae*. My translation.

69. An ancient symbol of self-reflexivity as well as of the eternal return, it was also used in alchemical illustrations to symbolize the circular nature of the alchemist's art.

70. The Biodôme is in Montréal, Canada. However, Magrelli entitled this section *Toronto, Ontario* because he liked the nursery rhyme sound of the two place names fused together.

71. Alberto Savinio, *Casa "La Vita"*. Milan, Adelphi, 1943. Savinio, Giorgio De Chirico's brother was an Italian writer and painter.

72. It is called "four seasons" because each 1/4 of the pizza has a topping which corresponds to a particular season of the year. The artichokes represent spring, the olives summer, the mushrooms fall, and the ham winter.

73. James Joyce, *Ulysses*, Episode 9, Scylla and Charybdis. London, Bodley Head, 1960.

74. A Pelele is a straw doll effigy. In Goya's painting the scarecrow is being tossed in a sheet.

75. Roberto Calasso, *The Ruins of Kasch*. Harvard, Belknap Press, 1996.

76. James Frazer, *The Golden Bough*. London, Macmillan, 1890

77. In the Italian the phrase is *capo del Capo*, with a play on words between the word *capo* (head) and the capitalized *Capo* meaning Boss.

78. Piazzale Loreto, Milan, April 28, 1945. The bodies of Benito Mussolini, Claretta Pettacci, and other Fascist leaders were hung by their feet after being shot.

79. "Mourant au XXe siècle d'une mort d'empereur du IIIe siècle." Marguerite Yourcenar, *Sans benefice d'inventaire*. Paris, Gallimard, 1978, p.34

80. In Roman Law this term refers to the extinguishing of a person's legal rights.

81. Umberto Saba, *Scorciatoie e raccontini*, Milan, Mondadori,1946

82. *Defences against Tyrants*. This Huguenot tract posed questions concerning the way people respond to their King.

83. Rater than be crucified like Jesus, Peter asked to be placed head down.

About the Author

Valerio Magrelli (Rome, 1957) is the author of six poetry collections, for which he has won among other prizes the Mondello, the Viareggio, the Montale and the Premio Antonio Feltrinelli-Accademia dei Lincei: *Ora serrata retinae* (Feltrinelli, 1980), *Nature e venature* (Mondadori, 1987), *Esercizi di tiptologia* (Mondadori, 1992), *Didascalie per la lettura di un giornale* (Einaudi, 1999), *Disturbi del sistema binario* (Einaudi, 2006), and *Il sangue amaro* (Einaudi, 2014). He has published four books of prose: *Nel condominio di carne* (Einaudi 2002), *La vicevita. Treni e viaggi in treno* (Laterza 2009), *Addio al calcio* (Einaudi 2010), and *Geologia di un padre* (Einaudi 2013), as well as critical studies on Dadaism, Paul Valéry, Charles Baudelaire and notable translations of Molière, Beaumarchais, Mallarmé, Verlaine, Debussy, Koltès, and Barthes.

A Professor of French literature at the University of Pisa and then Cassino, he is also a frequent contributor to the cultural pages of the Italian dailiy "La Repubblica." His poems have been translated into several languages. In English: *Nearsights: Selected Poems* (translated by A. Molino, Graywolf Press, 1991), *The Contagion of Matter* (Holmes & Meyer, 2000), *"Instructions on How to Read a Newspaper" and Other Poems* (Chelsea Editions, 2008), *The Embrace* (Faber & Faber, 2009; winner of the Oxford-Weidenfeld Prize and the John Florio Prize) and *Vanishing Points* (bilingual edition of *The Embrace*, Farrar, Straus and Giroux, 2010).

About the Translator

Clarissa Botsford has worked in the fields of teaching, intercultural education, editing, translating and publishing and is also a singer, violinist, and lay celebrant. She currently teaches English and Translation Studies at Rome University. In 2014, her translation of the novel *Sworn Virgin* by Elvira Dones was published by And Other Stories.

Free Verse Editions

Edited by Jon Thompson

13 ways of happily by Emily Carr
Between the Twilight and the Sky by Jennie Neighbors
Blood Orbits by Ger Killeen
The Bodies by Chris Sindt
The Book of Isaac by Aidan Semmens
Canticle of the Night Path by Jennifer Atkinson
Child in the Road by Cindy Savett
Condominium of the Flesh by Valerio Magrelli, trans. by Clarissa Botsford
Contrapuntal by Christopher Kondrich
Country Album by James Capozzi
The Curiosities by Brittany Perham
Current by Lisa Fishman
Dismantling the Angel by Eric Pankey
Divination Machine by F. Daniel Rzicznek
Erros by Morgan Lucas Schuldt
The Forever Notes by Ethel Rackin
The Flying House by Dawn-Michelle Baude
Instances: Selected Poems by Jeongrye Choi, translated by Brenda Hillman, Wayne de Fremery, & Jeongrye Choi
The Magnetic Brackets by Jesús Losada, translated by Michael Smith & Luis Ingelmo
A Map of Faring by Peter Riley
No Shape Bends the River So Long by Monica Berlin & Beth Marzoni
Pilgrimly by Siobhán Scarry
Physis by Nicolas Pesque, translated by Cole Swensen
Poems from above the Hill & Selected Work by Ashur Etwebi, translated by Brenda Hillman & Diallah Haidar
The Prison Poems by Miguel Hernández, translated by Michael Smith
Puppet Wardrobe by Daniel Tiffany
Quarry by Carolyn Guinzio
remanence by Boyer Rickel
Signs Following by Ger Killeen
Split the Crow by Sarah Sousa
Spine by Carolyn Guinzio
Spool by Matthew Cooperman
Summoned by Guillevic, translated by Monique Chefdor

Sunshine Wound by L. S. Klatt
These Beautiful Limits by Thomas Lisk
The Thinking Eye by Jennifer Atkinson
An Unchanging Blue: Selected Poems 1962–1975 by Rolf Dieter Brinkmann, translated by Mark Terrill
Under the Quick by Molly Bendall
Verge by Morgan Lucas Schuldt
The Wash by Adam Clay
We'll See by George Godeau, translated by Kathleen McGookey
What Stillness Illuminated by Yermiyahu Ahron Taub
Winter Journey [Viaggio d'inverno] by Attilio Bertolucci, translated by Nicholas Benson
Wonder Rooms by Allison Funk

www.ingramcontent.com/pod-product-compliance
Ingram Content Group UK Ltd.
Pitfield, Milton Keynes, MK11 3LW, UK
UKHW041643190726
13854UKWH00006B/2676